For Abrams:
Editor: Juliet Dore
Design Manager: Heesang Lee
Managing Editor: Amy Vinchesi
Production Manager: Larry Pekarek

Conceived, edited, and designed by Quarto Publishing, an imprint of The Quarto Group.

For Quarto:
Commissioning editor: Jo Lightfoot
Editor: Charlene Fernandes
Copyeditor: Claire Waite Brown
Design: Karin Skånberg
Designer: Eliana Holder
Illustrator: Thiago Corrêa
Production manager: David Hearn
Managing editor: Emma Harverson
Art director: Martina Calvio
Publisher: Lorraine Dickey

Library of Congress Control Number: 2025930355

ISBN: 978-1-4197-8076-9
eISBN: 978-8-88707-637-9

Copyright © 2025 Quarto Publishing plc
Illustrations copyright © 2025 Thiago Corrêa

Published in 2025 by Abrams, an imprint of ABRAMS. All rights reserved. No portion of this book may be reproduced, stored in a retrieval system, or transmitted in any form or by any means, mechanical, electronic, photocopying, recording, or otherwise, without written permission from the publisher.

Printed and bound in China
10 9 8 7 6 5 4 3 2 1

Abrams books are available at special discounts when purchased in quantity for premiums and promotions as well as fundraising or educational use. Special editions can also be created to specification. For details, contact specialsales@abramsbooks.com or the address below.

Abrams® is a registered trademark of Harry N. Abrams, Inc.

ABRAMS The Art of Books
195 Broadway, New York, NY 10007
abramsbooks.com

MYSTIC KITTY

A CAT'S GUIDE TO MEDITATION

VALERIE OULA
ILLUSTRATED BY THIAGO CORRÊA

ABRAMS, NEW YORK

CONTENTS

Introduction — 6

CHAPTER ONE
JUST OBSERVE — 8

Cat Teachings:
Feline Observations — 10
Breath Awareness — 12
Alternate Nostril Breathing — 14
Expanded Awareness &
Peripheral Vision — 16
Candle Gazing — 18
Sky Gazing — 20
Gazing Deeply — 22
Flower Gazing — 24
Kitty Gazing — 26
Appreciation & Gratitude — 28

CHAPTER TWO
JUST MEOW — 30

Cat Teachings:
Feline Frequencies — 32
Bee Breath — 34
Hissing Breath — 36
Throat Chakra — 38
Sound Healing — 40
Chanting — 42
Mantra — 44
Purr Vibrations — 46
Cat King Mudra — 48
Catch a Dove — 50

CHAPTER THREE
JUST PLAY — 52

Cat Teachings:
Feline Fun — 54
Jumping Jacks — 56
Catwalk — 58
Cat-Cow Asana — 60
Happy Kitten — 62
Kitty Curl and Arch — 64
Dance & Shake — 66
Lion's Breath — 68
Blowing Out the
Venom Breath — 70
Tiger Pose — 72
Paw Taps for Funsies — 74
Listen Up, Pussycats — 75

CHAPTER FOUR
JUST REST 76

Cat Teachings:
Catnaps	78
Box Breathing	80
Somatic Eye Press	82
Lunar Breath	84
Paws Out	86
Slow Blinks	88
Progressive Relaxation	90
Somatic Hug	92
Cool Cats Abound	94
Cat Wiggle	96

CHAPTER FIVE
JUST BE 98

Cat Teachings:
Copycat	100
No Doing, Just Being	102
Coherence Breathing	104
Elemental Being Breath	106
Inner Smile	108
Meowfulness Meditation	110
Loving Kittens Meditation	112
Bask in Love	114
Soothing Energy Head Hold	116
Mudra to Activate Feline Wisdom	118
Kitty Mudra	119

OUTRO
PARTING PURRS 120

Cat Teachings:
Paws & Pause	122
Ho'oponopono for Forgiveness	124
Lucky Cat Mewdra	125
Index	126
Acknowledgments	128

INTRODUCTION

If cultivating a meditation practice has always eluded you, and you love cats, you've been searching for this very book most of your life without even realizing it. We present to you a perfect pairing: cats and meditation.

Meditation not only helps to relieve stress and lower blood pressure and inflammation, it also increases brain function and slows aging by lengthening our telomeres—a DNA biomarker for longevity. Put simply, meditation makes us smarter and younger.

So why haven't you incorporated it into a daily practice yet? Does it feel hard or plain-old boring? Perhaps you just need the proper motivating factor, in which case I've got the perfect solution: you've guessed it, cats!

Simply looking at cat pictures can lower cortisol. If you are into cats, it can be that simple! Now, what if we were to look at or think about cats while we meditate? Whoa! Logic would say that should exponentially compound the health benefits.

In other words, it's time to reclaim the term "crazy cat lady" and repurpose it into "crazy-regulated-calm cat person"!

LUCKY CAT

You may be familiar with the ubiquitous statue of the lucky cat. With its one raised paw, it is seen in many Asian shops and restaurants, and is believed to attract prosperity and good luck. This little cat is usually white with red painted ears, although the figurines come in all kinds of colors, even black, pink, and gold.

The lucky cat originates in Japan, and its name, the *maneki-neko*, means "beckoning cat." There are a few origin stories for this feline, but the most famous version involves a nobleman in the fifteenth century and a white cat that beckoned him into a temple before a violent thunderstorm ensued. The nobleman was so impressed by the luck of this cat, that he became a patron of the temple, Gōtoku-ji in Tokyo, and helped to rebuild it in 1633. Today the temple is inundated with tourists year after year.

OUR FELINE INSPIRATION

We can invoke the lineage of the lucky cat to help guide us with our meditative inner journey to peace, calm, self-awareness, and abundance. To this end, this book features 50 practices where Mystic Kitty will inspire you to get started with meditation, which is usually half the battle. Flip through and choose a random practice to do daily, or start at the beginning and continue in order to the end, doing one practice a day, or more, to see which resonates with you.

TRY AGAIN

You may have seen Timo the ragdoll cat on YouTube. Timo's guardians got him a standing cat hammock, which he might have been a little too big for. Videos of Timo show him using various approaches to get into the hammock and famously failing over and over. And yet, he kept at it. Four months later, he finally finds the approach for success.

This story of big kitty vs small hammock reminds us that persistence and commitment are rewarded. And that is how we might approach our meditative practices. There are days we fall off and then we get right back to it, without judgment. Don't put pressure on yourself to get it right, or even get it at all! Instead, take that small spark of desire and intention and follow it.

WORDS OF ENCOURAGEMENT FROM MYSTIC KITTY

Mystic Kitty is here to support you, and the first and most important teaching is that you be like kitty and find delight and play in all that you do, including meditation. Here are some more words of advice from Mystic Kitty:

- Any time you see kitty's paws, remember to take a pause and breathe.
- Don't sweat the small stuff, play with it instead!
- Trust that you will always land on your feet, and you will.
- When in doubt, tilt your head to clear it out, and use your paw to knock something over!
- Live your life for no one else but you, just as cats do.
- It's such a short ride—slow down time through meowfulness and meditation to fully appreciate how sweet and playful life truly is, and come home to yourself.

CHAPTER ONE

JUST OBSERVE

We observe the world with our physical eyes, but we can also use our inner eye to observe our internal world. By tending to what's inside, we can affect what's outside. The easy breath and gazing techniques described in this chapter help hone our observation practices into contemplative gold while also calming the mind and releasing stress.

CAT TEACHINGS

FELINE OBSERVATIONS

So much learning among wild animals and humans comes from observation. Cats have a keen sense of observation, especially targeted toward hunting prey. The wild cat ancestor spotted an opportunity with this, grabbed it by the tail, and never looked back.

As civilizations moved from nomadic lifestyles to growing and storing food and grain, granaries became a horn of plenty for mice, which in turn attracted wild cats to the party. The wild cats and humans observed and recognized that this was a mutually beneficial relationship, and so it was that our sweet kitty's ancestors domesticated themselves, happily living alongside humans and becoming one of the most popular animal companions in the world.

Observation is key to wisdom—it is only through quiet observation that we can begin to map and track our external and, perhaps even more importantly, our internal world. There may be a part of us that is reluctant to begin quiet observation because we are afraid of what we might find within ourselves. What have we been avoiding facing? Some may find that they do not like themselves very much and either be motivated to make changes in their life or fall into a spiral of negativity. It's hard to imagine that our feline companions might ever start tearing themselves apart internally or start being critical about themselves (though we have all seen images of seemingly judgmental cats with a resting definitely-judging-you face!). We can learn so much from our cat companions simply being unapologetically who they are.

Just as simply as you can begin to observe, you can meditate. Meditation is observation; it's paying attention inwardly with intention. It invites us to cultivate a practice of observing ourselves and developing more self-awareness, which can lead to more satisfaction in life. What wisdom might we begin to reap in observing this present moment in time?

BREATH AWARENESS

*Without breath, there is no life. When we learn to bring awareness
to our breath, we can slow down and bring more appreciation into our lives.*

Cats breathe through their noses, and if you see them breathing through their mouths or panting, it's usually an indication that they are stressed or struggling to breathe. The same is true for humans. Stress and anxiety may cause you to breathe unconsciously through your mouth, which can then stress your system.

Lots of people inadvertently breathe through their mouths, so awareness and compassion are key to nonjudgmentally assessing how you are breathing. If you are breathing through your mouth, see this as an invitation to slowly change that habit mindfully and intentionally through observation. It might feel uncomfortable or even unnatural at first, but remember you are retraining a habit.

Ancient yogis believed that everyone came into this life with a finite number of breaths, and when that number is used up, that is the end of that lifetime. So it makes sense that most pranayama practices teach you how to slow your breath down. Pranayama in Sanskrit breaks down into *prana*, which means "life force energy" and *ayama*, meaning "regulation." With breath control practices, we can regulate our life force energy.

Diaphragmatic breathing involves breathing long and deep into the belly, and is the most efficient way to breathe. By allowing the diaphragm to move down, the lungs can expand to their fullest capacity, which means we get to access all the resources that breath has to offer.

This breath practice is contraindicated in pregnancy and for those with heart issues and high blood pressure.

Here is a practice to regulate our system through breath and create space for more life.

1. Sit in a comfortable upright position, or lie down with your knees up. Begin by taking a moment to pause.

2. If it is comfortable for you to do so, close your eyes, and if not, simply soften your gaze.

3. Feel how your body is supported at this moment. Spend a few seconds noticing how your breath moves in and out.

4. Bring your hands to rest lightly on your abdomen. With the next breath in, send it down to the abdomen and feel the expansion of your belly through your hands.

5. On the exhale, draw your navel back, feeling the contraction and squeezing all the air out.

6 Take your time to slowly repeat this practice. Start with a minimum of three minutes and slowly build to longer, learning and feeling what it is like to breathe long, slow, and deep.

7 To end, simply finish up the cycle of breath and allow your hands to come to rest. Let the breath be as it is and notice how you are feeling, being with whatever comes up without judgment.

4/8/8 EXERCISE

When we breathe in, we take in oxygen. When we breathe out, we release carbon dioxide. When we hold the breath out, we increase tolerance to carbon dioxide buildup and learn to regulate our breath in times of stress.

This example follows a count of 4/8/8, but if this is too difficult to begin with, start with 2/4/4 and build toward the full count.

- Following the steps for the above practice, inhale for a count of four.
- Exhale for a count of eight.
- Hold the breath out for a count of eight.
- Repeat for four slow rounds, gradually building to eight rounds.
- To end, do one last round and then come to rest.

ALTERNATE NOSTRIL BREATHING

Cats self-soothe by kneading their paws into a soft surface, alternating one little paw at a time in a reciprocal movement pattern. This action is reminiscent of when they nursed as kittens, and brings them comfort. How might we humans learn from this behavior to comfort ourselves?

One excellent self-soothing practice for adults is to breathe through alternate nostrils using a basic pranayama breath technique called nadi shodhana, meaning "channel clearing."

In traditional Indian medicine, the nadis are energetic channels that run throughout the body. There are said to be at least 72,000 of these channels where *prana*—life force energy—travels through the physical body, connecting at the chakras (energy centers). When you practice nadi shodhana, imagine that each breath in and out cleanses not only your nasal passageways but also your energetic channels, so that energy can flow more easily.

You might want to blow your nose before beginning alternate nostril breathing, and if you are a little stuffy in one nostril or another, this practice could help open your nasal passageways. You might also consider that if one nostril is blocked, perhaps something else is temporarily, energetically blocked. It could mean that some aspects in your life could use more flow. When the blocked nostril opens up physically, it may mean there is more receptivity in your body and flow in your life.

This practice can help to balance the left and right hemispheres of the brain and regulate the nervous system.

1 Sit upright and comfortably, with the left hand resting on the left leg, with the tips of the thumb and index finger touching (see Gyan Mudra, opposite).

2 Gently hold down the right nostril with the right thumb, with the remaining fingers pointing straight up. Inhale gently through the left nostril for a count of six and suspend the breath for a count of three.

3 Use the ring finger and/or pinky of the right hand to hold down the left nostril. Release the thumb and release the breath through the right nostril for a count of six. Adjust the count ratio to 2/1/2 depending on your comfort level. There should be no straining.

Breath retention or suspension is not recommended for anyone with high blood pressure.

14
JUST OBSERVE

4\. Inhale gently through the right nostril and suspend the breath as before. Hold down the right nostril with the thumb and release the breath through the left nostril. This is one full round.

5\. Repeat for a few more rounds, going at your own pace and taking time to slow, observe, and follow the breath. Start with three minutes and slowly build to longer durations.

6\. When you are ready to finish, complete the round. Release the hands to rest on your lap. And with eyes still closed, just be with the natural rhythm of your breath and notice the shifts in your body and mind.

GYAN MUDRA

The term "mudra" refers to "sealing" the fingers to maintain focus and direct energy. Gyan mudra is known across Buddhist and Hindu traditions as the mudra of wisdom, and when we hold this mudra we activate our system to receive wisdom.

EXPANDED AWARENESS & PERIPHERAL VISION

Cats have a much wider field of vision than humans. Their eyes are adapted to seeing in dim light and designed to spot rapid movement—all excellent for catching prey.

Oftentimes when we are stressed, we are either hyper-fixated on an issue or we are overwhelmed by everything and the opposite happens—we aren't able to focus at all. Tunnel vision or tunneled senses can happen under extreme stress, and anxiety arises because our peripheral vision and/or peripheral senses are lost in that moment. The solution is to step back and give yourself some space.

There's a wonderful Neuro Linguistic Programming (NLP) technique called Expanded Awareness, or Peripheral Vision Technique, which can really help us feel more centered. This technique seems to be based on an ancient Hawaiian Huna practice called Hakalau (*haka* translates as "to focus" and *lau* "to spread out"). As cats have a broader field of vision than we do, they can be said to have more perspective than humans. We can benefit by practicing what comes naturally to cats by extending and expanding our field of vision. This increases our sense of safety and activates our parasympathetic nervous system to rest and relax.

Here's a practice to expand your awareness and peripheral vision.

1 Find a place to sit comfortably. Close your eyes. Take a slow breath deeply in and even more slowly out.

2 Take time to notice all sounds, near and far. Notice if there's one sound that seems most obvious and allow yourself time to take in the sound. Notice the sound without needing to label it in any way; just allow it to be simply sound.

3 Begin to take in all the other sounds as well. Simply by opening your sensory awareness, listen and receive all the sounds near and far. Notice your breath. Notice how you are feeling in your body as you take in all the sounds. Don't strive to hear; simply allow the different sounds to enter your realm of awareness, one at a time, then layered, and then all at once. Notice the pockets of silence.

4 Start to shift your awareness to your gaze. Slowly opening your eyes, gently fix your gaze upon an object or spot directly in front of you. Take in that object or that spot with clear focus, then begin to soften your gaze, still remaining focused on your chosen spot or object. No straining, just allowing.

5 Now, slowly begin to widen your gaze without moving your eyes, as you gradually allow more and more into your peripheral vision. Breathing gently, allow your body to relax as your gaze softens and your awareness expands. Allow yourself to take in more, opening up to more of the top, bottom, and sides of your vision without moving your eyes.

6 Notice the sensations in your body: perhaps there's a warmth in your belly or throughout your body as you begin to release tension, a feeling of circulation. Notice how you might be seeing more of the space around you than you had before.

7 Take time to simply sit back and receive in this state of expanded and expansive awareness, allowing the breath to be slow and easy.

8 Allow your body to breathe normally again, knowing and remembering that you can always return to this place, this state of calm, by softening your focus and widening your vision, and breathing slow and steady.

17
EXPANDED AWARENESS & PERIPHERAL VISION

CANDLE GAZING

Have you ever challenged a cat to a staring contest? One where you see who can go the longest without blinking? Guaranteed, kitty wins and human loses.

Humans might blink 15 to 20 times a minute, whereas cats don't really need to blink at all since they have a third eyelid that helps to keep their eyes moist without really having to blink in the same way we do. While we can never outstare a feline friend, we can use the action of gazing to take ourselves into a meditative state.

The Sanskrit word *tratak* means "to gaze," and a trataka meditation is a yogic practice for focus and purification that is traditionally taught by concentrating on specific layers of color within the flame of a candle, without blinking. The eyes will tear, which is cleansing and purifying, and by fixing our gaze in this way we cleanse, calm, and stabilize our minds too.

Candle gazing has been known to help alleviate anxiety and stress as well as sharpen focus and concentration. It strengthens your physical eyes, as well as the intuitive "third" eye through the pineal gland.

Please make sure to trim the wick of your candle before lighting.

Place candle in a draft-free place.

Keep candle away from flammable materials.

Do not leave the candle unattended.

By gently stabilizing your gaze and breath, you can also stabilize your thoughts. Here we will practice a simplified, more accessible version of the trataka meditative technique.

1. In a dim or darkened room, place a candle about two feet in front of you at eye level, and sit comfortably in an upright position.

2. Set an intention for clarity and focus as you light the candle.

3. Close your eyes, if it is comfortable, or soften your gaze and look at the ground. Take a few gentle breaths in and out.

4. On the next breath in, send the breath down into your belly.

5. On the next breath out, slowly squeeze the air out, drawing your navel toward your spine.

6. When you are ready, open your eyes or lift your focus from the ground, soften your gaze, and stare at the light of the candle, noticing the movement of the flame.

7. Notice how your breath moves in and out and try to slow it down even more.

8. Slow and deepen each breath in and out as you continue to gaze at the wavering, flickering flame—you may notice the different colors within the flame.

9. Try to gaze at the flame without blinking as much as usual. Your eyes may begin to tear up.

10. If your eyes begin to tire, close them and focus through closed eyes, seeing the flame in your mind's eye.

11. You can continue this practice by doing a few minutes daily, beginning with three minutes and building up to 11 minutes maximum to protect the eyes from retinal damage.

12. When you are ready to end, simply give thanks to the fire element for burning and alchemizing your mind chatter, and blow the candle out.

19
CANDLE GAZING

SKY GAZING

Felines are such charming creatures that they have long inspired humans to name celestial discoveries after them. Cosmic cats shining in the night sky include the constellations of Leo, Leo Minor, even Lynx. There's also the Cat's Paw Nebula, the Cat's Eye Nebula, and the Cheshire Cat galaxies. The latest celestial kitty discovery, the Smiling Cat Nebula, is a stellar nursery that resembles a feline with a wide smile.

Whether or not you can see these cosmic lights named after cats, you can still contemplate the sky, a wonderful practice to connect to nature outside of you and at the same time with nature within you.

Sky gazing is a meditative practice that has its roots in Tibetan Buddhism. When we look up at the sky we might roll our eyes upward, which has the effect of producing alpha brain waves that help us to stay relaxed and focused, as well as strengthening creativity and intuition.

We also notice clouds coming and going and, in this practice, we remind ourselves that we are like the sky: at the heart of who we are is an expansive, boundless, sky-like being.

During this practice, as you gaze at the expansive sky, know that your essential nature is much like it: wide, vast, and limitless.

1. Choose a time of day that isn't too bright, such as early morning or at dusk, ideally when the sun isn't glaring out. Find a comfortable position outdoors, where you can look up at the sky. You can also practice indoors, if you have a place you can look upon the sky unobstructed. Sit upright in a comfortable position or lie down.

2. Close your eyes and take a gentle breath in through your nose and out through your mouth.

3. With your eyes still closed, roll your eyeballs toward the top of your head. Noticing your breath, keep the eyes rolled upward for no more than eight seconds, since they will tire easily. This action will help to produce alpha brain waves.

4. When you are ready, slowly open your eyes and maintain a soft gaze as you take in the sky. Notice the play and subtleties of color, and the clouds and their various shapes.

5. Take a few slow breaths in and out, keeping them soft and gentle as you watch the clouds, noticing their different formations. Consider what's obvious and then tune into the subtleties of the sky.

6. Take gentle in and out breaths as you continue to gaze and feel into being the sky. Remember your expansiveness.

7. On your next breath, breathe in the sky and, as you breathe out, breathe out the clouds. Breathe in your boundless being and breathe out distraction, anything that is not essential to your being.

8. Come back again and again to your inherent boundless nature. Remember, you are the sky. Everything else is the clouds and weather.

9. Continue at your own pace for as long as it feels comfortable.

10. When you are ready to end the meditation, simply close your eyes, breathe deeply, and give thanks to the sky and to your own infinite being.

SKY GAZING

GAZING DEEPLY

Have you ever considered what a cat might be thinking when it's staring at you? Perhaps it's close to feeding time and they are staring at you longingly or demandingly, hoping that you'll finally put food in their dish. Or maybe they are simply gazing at you as they begin to fall asleep because they feel safe and so very relaxed, blinking slowly to show their affection and trust.

Eye gazing is a practice common within Sufi contemplative meditations and involves sitting across from another person and gazing into one another's eyes. It can be an interesting and somewhat uncomfortable process, but we get to see ourselves literally reflected through another's eyes.

This can also be done alone in front of a mirror, which is the practice that we will share here. This is an invitation to meet yourself wherever you are. Know that perception is not truth, it's simply how we see the thing, and when we shift the way we see things, those things can change.

There are contraindications for anyone with body dysmorphia and anxiety.

This is a practice of softening and connection through which you can send love and compassion to the person in the mirror, who is doing the best they can with what they've got, and that is more than enough.

1. Make yourself comfortable in front of a mirror.

2. Soften your gaze as you look into your own eyes.

3. Take a few moments to consider:

- How you might connect to yourself more deeply
- How you might see yourself through your own eyes
- What is conscious and unconscious to your being?
- What is being reflected back to you as you soften your breath and breathe more fully and deeply while gazing at your reflection?

4. Notice what comes up as you breathe slowly and gaze into your own eyes. Allow any harsh critique to arise and let it move through, simply acknowledging that it can rise up, move through, and move out.

5. As you gaze, you can use your breath to soften the hard edges of your being. Try to connect to compassion within yourself for this "person" gazing back at you.

6. Continue gazing, breathing, and being with the person that you see, noticing all that you are without judgment.

7. Look into each eye for a few breaths, seeing and receiving, being and breathing, slow and deep. Continue for three minutes, building to five minutes. If it feels uncomfortable at any point, stop. When you are ready to end, thank yourself for showing up for yourself.

FLOWER GAZING

Images of pretty flowers, or cute cats, or, even better, cute cats in a field of flowers, are a surefire dopamine hit for the brain. When we are feeling good, we can appreciate more in our lives, and gratitude is definitely the way to inner peace.

In the Chinese philosophy and religion of Taoism, Tao refers to the fundamental way of the universe. The underlying principle is that all should be done in the flow to be in harmony and in balance with the universe. Cute cats sniffing pretty flowers might feel very much like harmony in the universe for some—according to the Instagram algorithm at least.

Here's a practice to connect us to the nature and beauty around and within us.

1. Whether you are indoors or outdoors, choose a single flower as your object of meditation. If you don't have access to a flower, pull up a picture of one to gaze upon.

2. Take a comfortable seat in front of the flower. With a gentle breath in and out, gaze at the flower before you, noticing the shapes of the leaves and petals.

3. Take in the scent of the flower or imagine what the scent might be. Breathe in and receive.

4. Notice the arrangements of the petals, the array of textures, colors, and subtleties within the flower and leaves, breathing slowly.

5. Breathing even more slowly, notice the play of light upon the flower and leaves. What else are you noticing about this flower?

6. As you gaze upon the flower, can you see it as a mirror? As you receive the energy, beauty, and imagined perfume of this flower, what might it be reflecting back to you?

7. Now, if it feels good to do so, close your eyes and imagine the flower in your mind's eye. See the colors and shapes through closed eyes.

8. Begin to listen. Listen to what this floral being wants to share with you. What beauty and wonder is this flower reminding you of within yourself? This flower is simply being, no striving and no needing to be anything other than how it is now.

9. Recognize the natural energy activated within you by simply gazing upon nature's beauty, every cell in your being remembering the beauty of its natural state. Take as much time as you need to simply sit and breathe and be.

10. When you are ready to end this interaction, give thanks in any way that feels best. Then, open your eyes.

KITTY GAZING

Of all the gazing meditations, choosing to focus on a delightful being of natural inspiration may well be your favorite. We are talking, of course, of cat gazing.

It would not be much of a stretch to assume, because you have chosen this book to inspire your meditations, that you are a lover or admirer of cats, and more than likely have access to a kitty to practice gazing upon. Don't worry if not, however, since there are other ways to meditate in admiration, including using the image on the opposite page as your object of focus.

The benefits of this practice are comparable to those of other meditations in that you'll experience lowered blood pressure and perhaps feel a sense of calm. This one specifically, however, may induce even more joy, so proceed with caution!

In this practice we will use a kitty as our object of focus, such as a sleeping cat or cat at rest, whether in real life or an image from this book.

1. Sit in front of a resting cat or image of a sleepy cat at an easy distance to gaze.

2. If it is comfortable for you to do so, close your eyes. Gently inhale and exhale, noticing how the breath moves in and out of your body.

3. When you are ready, open your eyes to gently gaze at the cat. Receive the energy of the colors, textures, and all that you are noticing about this animal.

4. Take this time to notice the shape that the cat makes as it rests. Notice the gentle respiration and movement of breath through the kitty, or simply imagine how breath moves.

5. Still gazing softly, scan the animal, starting from the tips of the ears, noticing the eyes, the little nose pad, the whiskers, and mouth. Consider the body, paws, and tail.

6. See if you can allow your eyes to soften as you gaze upon the softness of this creature.

7. As you continue to gaze at the feline, allow yourself to breathe slowly and deeply. Take as much time as you need to zoom in to one aspect of color in the fur, or perhaps the variation in texture on the cat's coat, then widen your gaze to take in the full shape of the animal. Notice, without judgment, what you sense when you gaze upon this cat.

8. Continue for three minutes and slowly build to longer if that feels good. When you are ready to finish the meditation, close your eyes and visualize in your mind's eye this resting cat, and feel that peace.

APPRECIATION & GRATITUDE

Have you ever been headbutted by a kitty? Or experienced a little body rub against your leg? Chalk it up to kitty appreciation and gratitude!

Technically, your furry friend is actually rubbing you with pheromones, most likely "marking" you as safe and familiar, but it feels more like they are telling you they appreciate you feeding them, or are grateful that you came home to them.

We humans should all be so thoughtful in our expression of appreciation and gratitude. Studies have shown time and again that tuning in to gratitude can positively affect our overall wellbeing, and can help us to feel more connected and happier in life.

We probably already realize that we should be grateful for what we have, but do we put that into practice in a way that is meaningful and impactful for our body and energy system? It is so easy to take what we have for granted. We don't know what we have until we no longer have it, and then the gratitude floods in 200 percent.

This practice is an invitation to really drop into true gratitude, which often begins with appreciation. Gratitude shifts our focus and energy to what we already have, and provides a sense of completeness that opens the floodgates for more in our lives.

The heart has an infinite capacity for appreciation and gratitude, and by tuning in to more of both we can feel happier and recognize how much we already have. Which, in turn, opens the doors for us to receive even more.

1. Sit comfortably with the hands on the heart, one on top of the other. This is an invitation to connect to your heart space, to your beautiful beating organ that holds so much.

2. Close your eyes if you are comfortable to do so, otherwise soften your gaze.

3. Remind yourself that each breath in and each breath out is a blessing, a blessing of the vital life force energy, prana.

4. Continue to bless yourself with breath, knowing that as your breath moves in and out, it brings nourishment to body, mind, and spirit.

5. As you continue to bless yourself with intentional and mindful breath, hands still connected to the heart space, bring to your mind's eye all that you are truly grateful for. Try to not think of what you "should" be grateful for, instead let it be true, which you'll know by the feeling in your gut.

6. Connect to three things right now that you are grateful for, and notice how that feels at your heart and in your body. Notice the sensations and allow that sense of pure gratitude to bring an image to your mind's eye, or perhaps just imagine a color that represents your gratitude.

7. Imagine, see, taste, and touch what gratitude feels like, employing all of your senses to make it as real as possible. Tune in and take as much time as you like to revel in this gratitude.

8. From this place of gratitude you might begin to connect to appreciation for an arduous situation, time, or relationship. Appreciation is what we might bring to a more challenging situation. You may not have gratitude for the thing yet, or ever, but what can you appreciate now in terms of wisdom, having lived through, or perhaps still in, the experience?

9. Spend some time breathing slowly and see what arises. Trust that this is a practice to help open your body, and soften your system to receive from a place of surrender, to heal and receive beyond what we know. Sit for three to five minutes and, if this practice resonates, build to 15 minutes.

10. When this practice feels complete, bring your hands to prayer and give thanks to yourself for taking this time to move you in the direction of more happiness.

CHAPTER TWO
JUST MEOW

Find your voice, express yourself, and speak your truth. In this chapter we will explore ways to create and receive sounds that connect the physical with the universal, consider the vibrational medicine of frequency and breath, and learn how these practices help to regulate the nervous system so that we can live authentically.

FELINE FREQUENCIES

It is said that cats have learned to meow as a way of interacting with humans, and that meows are exclusively used for this purpose. However, videos capturing the hidden life of cats taken with little portable cameras, often attached to the kitty's collar, reveal that, along with the general inter-cat communication of chirps, trills, and murmurs, much meowing also goes on.

Much like the sounds cats make to communicate among themselves, we humans have a few of our own that are pleasing to our feline companions. If you've been lucky enough to have had a cat in your life, at one point or another, you will know that the sound *pspspsps* seems to be the universal call for cats. Pet guardians often use *pspspsps* to call a cat home or, at the very least, to get their attention. But why is this sound so irresistible to felines?

Cats have extremely sensitive hearing. You might be *pspspsps*-ing from the kitchen and they will be roused from slumber deep inside the bedroom closet and come running! They can hear wide ranges and up to much higher frequencies than humans. So don't fret when your kitty companion stares intently at a wall as if something is there. It's probably not a ghost, but a noise they've heard.

When we use the combination of sounds and frequencies in *pspspsps*, we may inadvertently be mimicking the sound of prey rustling in the leaves, which piques their curiosity and draws their attention to us. Of course there is always the possibility that the call of *pspspsps* is accompanied by the giving of food—dinner time!—therefore becoming a sound associated with a treat.

Both of these explanations can be applied to humans, in that we can use sound for ourselves, for example through anchoring the sound of a mantra with a state of calm! With repetition, we can use sound and frequencies to shift our state of being.

BEE BREATH

A cat's purr is self-soothing and balances the system. In a similar way, humming in humans can be very beneficial to the parasympathetic nervous system. Bhramari pranayama, also known as Bee Breath, is a breathing technique that involves humming as it resembles the sound of a bee.

Bhramari is the name of a black bumble bee in India and is also Sanskrit for "bee." The practice of bee breathing has so many benefits! It's been known to help with anxiety, depression, and rumination. The internal humming sounds can quiet the mind, clearing any extraneous energy, while the frequency of the hum helps to bring more coherence into the body by balancing heart rate and respiration and regulating the nervous system.

Humming is a tool that we can access at almost any time. The more you bring humming into your daily life, the better the results.

This exercise should not be practiced during menstruation or pregnancy. Also contraindicated for high blood pressure, epilepsy, chest pain, or an ear infection. Please do not practice lying down.

Before you begin, locate the tragus, the little flap of cartilage by your ears on the sides of the cheeks.

1. Sit in a comfortable upright position with eyes closed, if you wish. Breathe slowly and deeply. Position a thumb on each tragus, with the fingers resting on the head.

2. Gently inhale through the nose. Exhale through the nose with a closed mouth, and make a low, continuous hum, like the buzzing of a bee, until you need to inhale. This is one round.

3. Continue for a few more rounds, noticing what you are aware of as you continue to breathe and hum.

4. With subsequent inhales, know that you are taking in more breath, more life force energy. With subsequent exhales, tune in to the vibrations in your face and head as you hum.

5. Keep your focus on the humming sound and recognize that it is balancing your mind and body. We are vibrational beings. Everything, down to its smallest molecular component, is vibrating. Everything is frequency, and when we hum we can balance the frequency in our bodies as well as in our lives.

6. Practice for three to five minutes.

7. When you are done, with the eyes still closed, release the hands down to rest and simply sit for a while and just be.

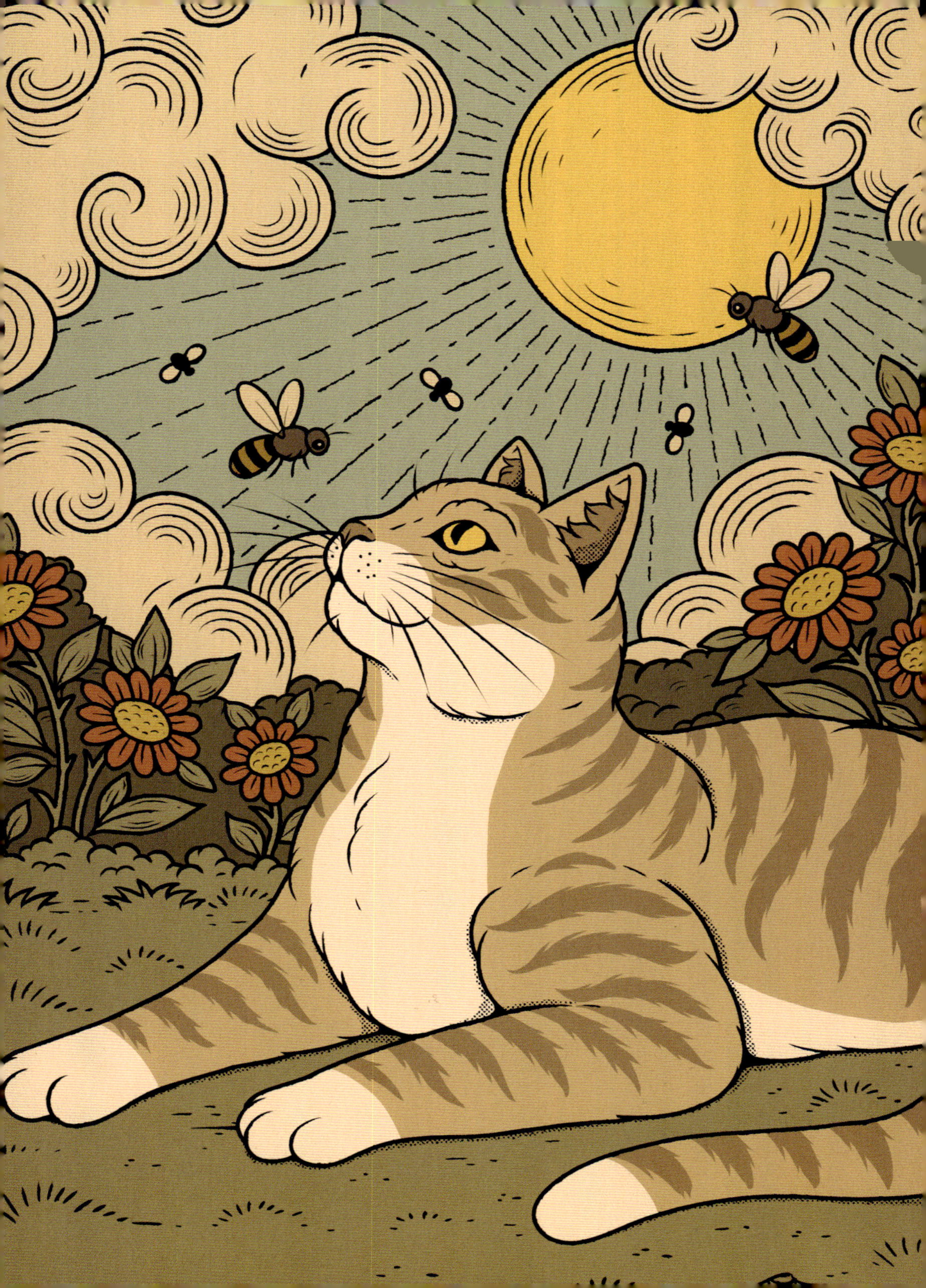

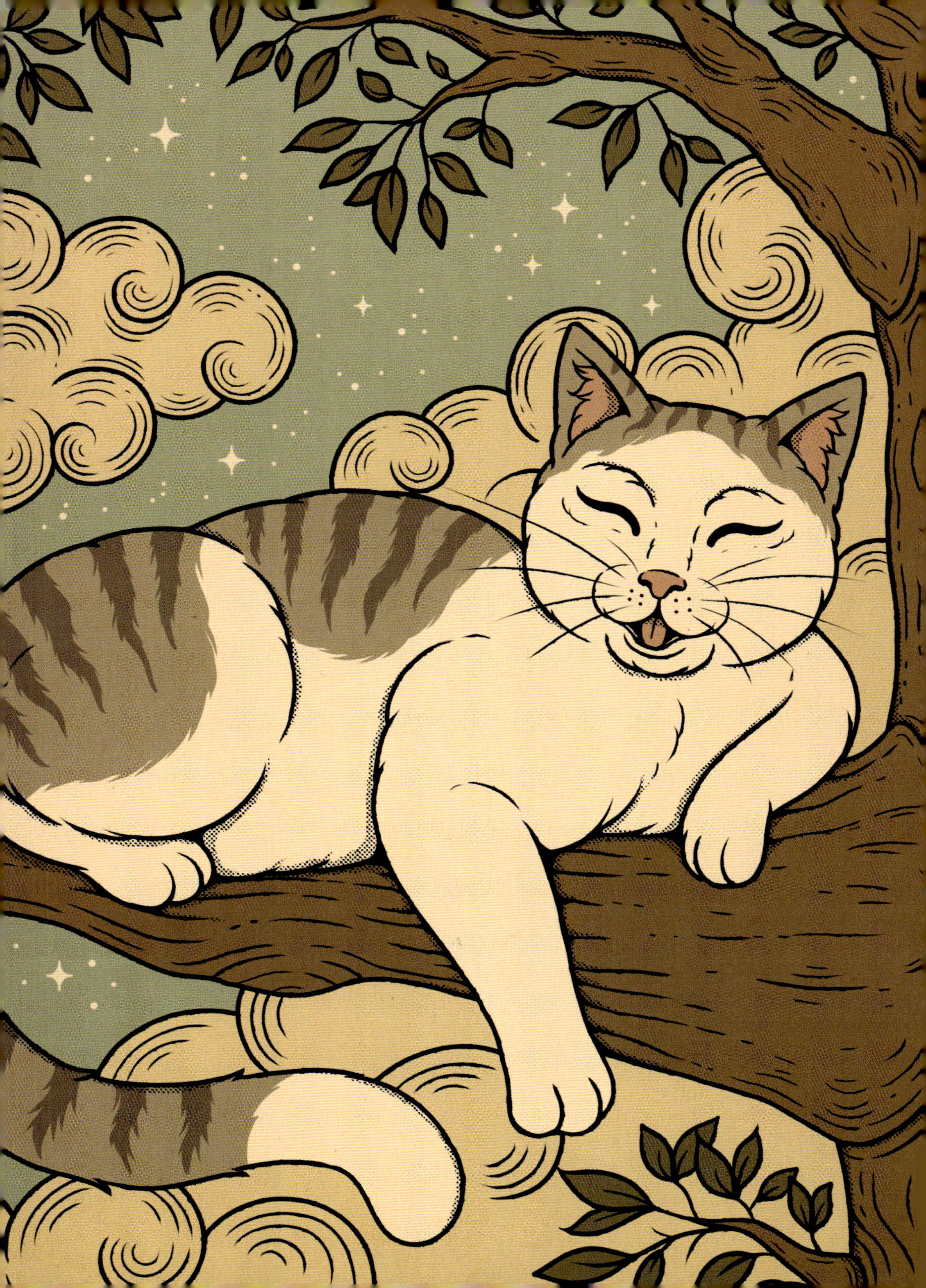

HISSING BREATH

Cats hiss when they are threatened or frightened, as a warning and in the hope that a good hiss is enough to prevent further escalation—they would prefer to avoid confrontation.

Sitkari refers to the hissing sound in Sanskrit, and we might use this breath practice in a similar way to the feline response, to calm the mind and emotions, especially when angry and heated. It's an excellent cooling breath for navigating tricky situations where you might naturally want to hiss at everyone anyway!

This hissing breath is super simple to practice and may also help with insomnia, perimenopausal/menopausal hot flashes, hypertension, digestive issues, mental clarity, and so much more.

This breath practice is contraindicated for those who experience low blood pressure, migraines, or heart issues.

With each hissing inhale, imagine it cooling and calming your body as well as your mind. With each breath out, imagine moving excess heat from the body and mind, releasing any stress, anger, and anxiety.

1. Sit in a comfortable upright position with eyes closed, if you wish. Rest the hands on the thighs or knees and take a few gentle breaths in and out.

2. Bring the tip of your tongue to the upper palate, allowing it to rest behind the front teeth. Let the top and bottom teeth lightly touch, with the lips parted.

3. On the inhale, sip the breath in through the teeth, making a hissing sound as the breath moves in and feeling a cooling sensation as it moves through the teeth and over the tongue.

4. On the exhale, release the tongue and teeth, close the lips, and release the breath through your nose. This is one full round.

5. As you continue at a slow, steady pace, feel the cooling breath that you are drawing into your body with each inhale through the teeth. With each exhale through the nose, allow yourself to clear out any heated emotions in your mind and body.

6. Continue this practice, starting with one minute and building up to three minutes or more to allow your nervous system to begin to regulate.

7. When you have completed the final round of breath, take a moment to sit quietly, noticing what you are feeling and what's shifted for you.

THROAT CHAKRA

Do you find yourself in situations where the "cat has got your tongue"? Tuning in to your throat chakra can help you to work through these awkward moments.

According to many eastern traditions, the chakras are energy centers along the body that bridge energy from the outer world into our inner world, and vice versa. These energy centers correspond to specific nerve bundles within the body. When our chakras are balanced, energy flows. Any imbalances and blocks in the energy centers show up in the physical and emotional body.

The throat chakra is associated with truth and communication, and is also the chakra related to creative expression.

Seed mantras—also known as bija mantras—are monosyllabic words believed to help activate their corresponding chakras. Using seed sounds helps us to cleanse and balance a chakra so that energy may flow freely. The seed mantra for the throat is "ham."

A few ways to balance your throat chakra include:
- Humming and/or singing out loud
- Meditating with blue-colored gemstones or crystals such as aquamarine, blue topaz, turquoise, amazonite, or celestite
- Wearing blue gemstones and crystal earrings or a necklace
- Chanting aloud, especially the seed syllable "ham," to open and strengthen the flow of energy through this chakra

Blue is the color of the throat chakra. Visualizing the color blue and sensing what the blue feels like bolsters this energy center. The more you practice visualizing the power of blue light and energy at your throat, the more empowered you will be to express your truth and creativity.

1. Sit in a comfortable upright position and rub the palms of your hands together a few times to create some heat.

2. Bring your hands to gently hold/cup the throat in an easy, relaxed manner, without tension or strain.

3. Close your eyes, if that's comfortable, and breathe normally. Feel the warmth of your hands and the energy imparted from them, soothing your throat and neck. Feel your hands sharing comfort and support.

4. Bringing a soft focus to your throat and in your mind's eye, direct your attention and energy to your throat chakra. Notice whatever it is you are feeling as you softly hold your awareness at your throat. If you need to, lower your hands down to rest at any point.

5. Now visualize the color blue. Notice what shade of blue it is. Is it light or dark? See the blue as a kind of light or energy.

6. Allow the blue color to expand through your throat and neck, then from there to the rest of your body.

7. With the next breath in and out, imagine this blue energy is the color of your truth and creative expression. Notice what happens to the blue energy as you continue to breathe long and deep. And as you allow the blue to expand, inhale deeply and chant out loud the throat chakra mantra, "ham," which sounds like "hum," as many times as you can in one breath and inhale again to chant, doing two more cycles. As you chant, feel the vibration on your lips and in your throat, and continue to visualize the color blue.

8. Take as much time as you wish to soak in the blue. When you are ready to end, give thanks for all that you have received consciously or unconsciously.

39
THROAT CHAKRA

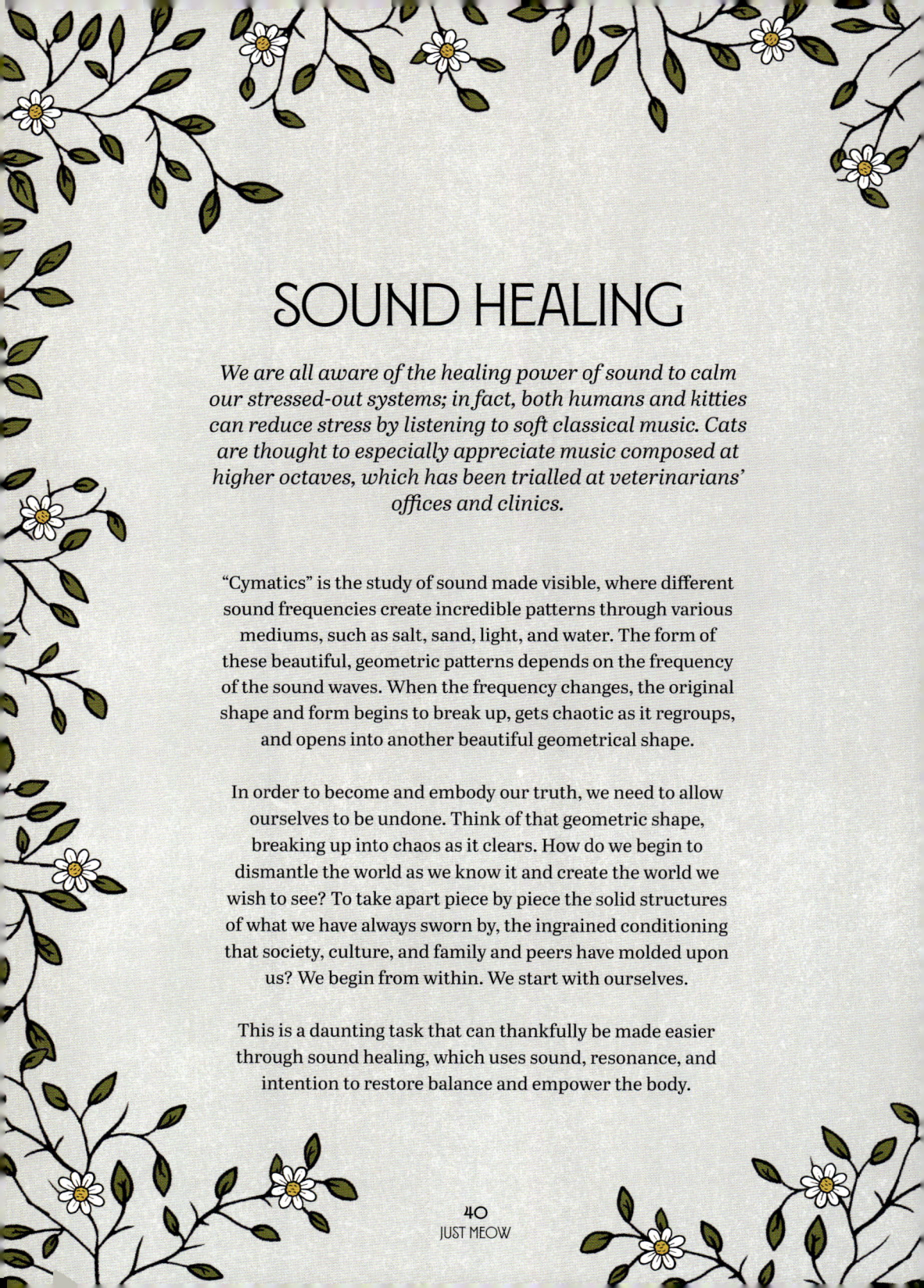

SOUND HEALING

We are all aware of the healing power of sound to calm our stressed-out systems; in fact, both humans and kitties can reduce stress by listening to soft classical music. Cats are thought to especially appreciate music composed at higher octaves, which has been trialled at veterinarians' offices and clinics.

"Cymatics" is the study of sound made visible, where different sound frequencies create incredible patterns through various mediums, such as salt, sand, light, and water. The form of these beautiful, geometric patterns depends on the frequency of the sound waves. When the frequency changes, the original shape and form begins to break up, gets chaotic as it regroups, and opens into another beautiful geometrical shape.

In order to become and embody our truth, we need to allow ourselves to be undone. Think of that geometric shape, breaking up into chaos as it clears. How do we begin to dismantle the world as we know it and create the world we wish to see? To take apart piece by piece the solid structures of what we have always sworn by, the ingrained conditioning that society, culture, and family and peers have molded upon us? We begin from within. We start with ourselves.

This is a daunting task that can thankfully be made easier through sound healing, which uses sound, resonance, and intention to restore balance and empower the body.

Attending group sound baths is incredible if you can do it, but in the meantime there are natural sources of sound healing that you might tune in to as well, such as birdsong or rain, the consistent sound of which can soothe and regulate the nervous system.

1 Source some audio recordings of birdsong or rain, or birds singing in the rain, such as tropical rainforest sounds. Set your chosen sound file to play on repeat.

2 Lie down and gently focus on your breath, with each breath helping your body to sink in and sink down.

3 Allow all the sounds, near and far, to be a part of your experience, soothing, balancing, restoring, and nourishing your mind, body, and spirit.

4 As you take in the sounds, you may notice:

- Each breath in as welcoming relaxation, and each breath out as releasing tension
- Each breath in bringing in balance, and each breath out letting go
- All is well as the birds sing their melodious sounds.
- All is well as the rain pours down upon the earth.
- All is well as you continue to breathe and receive.

5 Trusting that all is now restored, take as much time as you need to feel and breathe nature all around you and within you.

6 When you are ready to end the meditation, simply give thanks to those beautiful sounds of nature and bring your awareness back into the space.

CHANTING

Have you ever heard a cat caterwaul? It's different from a basic meow. It's yowling, and its point is to be loud. There are lots of reasons to yowl, from being hungry and bored, to a mating call, or due to confusion in old age. Humans can learn to caterwaul in a more positive and beneficial way; we can call it chanting.

When we can delve into the various subtle layers of our being, the world opens in miraculous and wondrous ways. Chanting sacred syllables activates what's sacred within us. How do we create, not find, the courage to live clear and true? We can begin by using our voices to chant in order to give ourselves the courage to express our truth loudly.

When we chant, we move our mouths to make sounds and prayers that have been sacred for centuries. We initiate our parasympathetic nervous system to rest and digest. We become a part of that collective energy through lineages of ancient traditions, chanting the same sounds and vibrations over and over again through the centuries. We become a part of that becoming, that embodying of the divine through sound.

This practice will introduce a simple phrase with four words as a variation on a traditional mantra which is Sanskrit in origin and is the sacred language of Hinduism, Buddhism, and Jainism. We will also use a mudra, a method of squeezing the fingers that essentially anchors a feeling into the body. In Yogic traditions, mudras activate energy through the body to support our intentions.

1. Sit in a comfortable upright position with your hands resting on your thighs, palms facing up.

2. Close your eyes, if that's comfortable, and if not, simply soften your gaze toward the ground.

3. Squeeze the fingers lightly on both hands together starting with the thumb to index finger, then thumb to middle finger, then thumb to ring finger, then thumb to pinky, then starting the cycle again back at the beginning.

4. Choose one of these phrases, or perhaps another four-word phrase, or just four words that you want to embody more of in your life:

I am embodied peace.
I am pure love.
I am pure peace.
Focused, calm, and blissful.
Courage, peace, love, strength.

5. Follow this pattern:
- Chant the words out loud as you squeeze the fingers for three rounds.
- Chant the words in a whisper as you squeeze the fingers for three rounds.
- Mentally chant the words as you squeeze the fingers for three rounds.

6. You can repeat all three rounds if you'd like to continue for longer.

7. When you are ready to end this practice, bring the hands to prayer and close out in gratitude.

MANTRA

Can the word cat *or the phrase "I adore cats!" count as a mantra, of sorts, if it interrupts your overthinking, anxiety-filled brain? Mystic Kitty says absolutely!*

From the Sanskrit for "mind" and "tool," mantras have long been used in Hinduism and Buddhism as a way of focusing on what we want and disrupting thoughts of what we don't want. It's like a deliberate, beneficial earworm!

Mantra is repetition of a sound, word, or phrase, and is a tool used in devotional chanting, most commonly a Sanskrit phrase from the Hindu or Buddhist traditions as a point of focus. The thing we hear repeatedly becomes ingrained in our minds and contributes to and creates the reality we perceive. Affirming the mantra in your head is a self-reprogramming of your brain.

Negative thoughts are a habit, and these repetitive thoughts you broadcast to your internal world can become the reality in your external world. With mindfulness and awareness we can be intentional about what we'd like to do differently, including shifting our thoughts so that what we focus on, what we direct our energy toward, grows.

There are many mantras that you can research online, words and phrases that have been used throughout history in various traditions to invite mental clarity and calm. You could also choose simple but potent words like *love* if it strongly resonates in your body. For example, you could focus on the word *cat* and see how it shifts your energy and state of being!

Mantras can be repeated any time of day, chanting out loud or mentally, the more often the better. And the way you choose to work with mantras is completely up to you, including finding words, affirmations, and sacred chants that best suit you.

In this example we use "so hum," the universal mantra meaning "I am that," which has a cleansing and restorative effect.

1 Sit in an upright, comfortable position, with eyes closed, if you wish.

2 With each slow breath in, mentally inhale "so."

3. With each slow breath out, mentally exhale "hum." You might begin to hear "so" as you breathe in, long and deep, and naturally hear "hum" as you breathe out, long and slow.

4. Continue for three minutes or more, focusing on the mantra.

5. When you are ready to end, finish out the cycle of breath. Take a moment to sit still and notice how you felt before and how you've shifted now. Bring the hands to prayer and give thanks.

PURR VIBRATIONS

You might say that kitties are the ultimate sound-healing facilitators. That sweet purr that sounds like a little motor running is filled with healing benefits, something that humans can replicate for themselves simply through humming.

Cats purr when they are content, although they may also purr when they aren't feeling well as a way of calming themselves. Purring activates the cat's vagus nerve, which is instrumental to regulating the nervous system when distressed. The frequency of a purr has been shown to correspond to frequencies that help heal broken bones, reduce inflammation, and encourage tissue regeneration.

The vibration of a cat's purr is calming and soothing for humans as well, but if you haven't got a cat on hand, you can use your own form of purr, by humming, to reduce stress, ground and elevate your energy, breathe easier, and open up your sinuses. Humming slows the heart rate, lowers your blood pressure, and revitalizes your cells and energy.

Humming is an excellent way to relax by stimulating and strengthening the vagus nerve. The beauty of humming is that you can do it anywhere, and will gain even more benefits by making it an intentional and regular practice.

1. Choose a comfortable position; this might be seated, lying down, or partially reclined.

2. Take some time to breathe into your body as you close your eyes. Take a gentle breath in and out and scan through your body, noticing where there might be tension or other sensations calling to you.

3. Take a longer, deeper breath in and begin to hum. You might hum a melody that's familiar to you, or hum your own melody with whatever tones come to you.

4. As you hum, move your mouth into a smile. Imagine that the sound and vibration you are making begins to open spaciousness in your body, system, and life. Feel the humming move through your body, releasing any tension.

5. Now imagine that your hum is sweeping up anything stale or stagnant within your body, dissolving any stress, overwhelm, or confusion, helping you to shift your way of thinking and energy.

6. As you continue to hum, know that you are creating more clarity in your body, system, and life. You are using your own sound to facilitate a sound bath, your own sound clearing.

7. When you are ready to close the meditation, bring one hand to the heart and the other hand to the belly or solar plexus, connecting you to your body, and finishing with gratitude for all.

CAT KING MUDRA

Did you know that in China, Elvis Presley is referred to as the king of cats? Perhaps because of his slick moves, or because he was graceful and oh-so handsome, but to the Chinese he is the ultimate king cat. How might we embody some of the cat king's ways?

We could start crooning "You ain't nothin' but a hound dog" every day in the shower but that is unlikely to give you that sense of confidence that Elvis exuded. Instead, we present to you the cat king mudra, also known as thunderbolt mudra or vajrapradama mudra. The Sanskrit word *vajra* means "thunderbolt" or "diamond," and according to Buddhist tradition the thunderbolt/diamond cuts through doubt and brings energy to the heart space that instils trust and confidence there.

This practice is a blend of mudra and a bija seed mantra for the heart chakra (the sound "yam") to build inner power, strengthen the heart, and restore trust and faith.

While the instructions given for this practice call for you to sit, this exercise can be carried out standing, sitting, or lying down. Of course, you can also practice the mudra and mantra separately if you wish.

1. Sit comfortably in an upright position, with the eyes closed or softly gazing downward. Roll the shoulders back and down.

2. Place your hands horizontally in front of your chest with palms facing you and fingers spread wide. Interweave the fingers of both hands so that the middle fingers intersect at the mid-section of the fingers, pointing out to opposite sides. Rest the right index finger on the nail of the left index finger with the thumbs pointing upward. You can place this mudra to rest on the chest or just in front of it, connecting with the heart space. Relax the elbows down and breathe slow, and deep.

3. Take a gentle breath in and start chanting the mantra "yam," which sounds like "yum" and is the sound of the heart chakra energy center. Take your time drawing out the sound and feeling the vibration that's created at your heart space. Repeat until you need to take another breath, then inhale and begin again.

4. Practice this mudra and mantra for three minutes and, as you do so, imagine that diamond and thunderbolt energy cutting through and clarifying doubt, fear, and ignorance in your body and system. Feel that you are being infused with internal power and radiance through breath, sound, and mudra. Over time you can increase your practice time to 11 minutes.

5 When you are ready to end, inhale and hold the breath lightly as the energy radiates through your whole body and being, then exhale. Release the mudra and allow the hands to come to rest. Take a few moment to observe the different shifts in your body.

CATCH A DOVE

The chitter-chatter sound of "ack ack ack ack" when kitty spots a bird is a form of mimicry, calling to their prey in hopes of ensnaring them with furry paws, sharp claws, and deadly teeth. This psychological cunning makes our felines formidable predators, and a gentle dove is no match for our domestic apex predator.

In this practice we can mimic kitty hunters with a dove in hand, minus the destruction but instead activating peace through kapota mudra and mantra. *Kapota* means "white dove" in Sanskrit, and this mudra calms body, mind, and spirit. The mantra paired with the mudra in this exercise is "om shanti om." *Om* is the sacred sound of the universe and *shanti* means "peace." When we chant this mantra, we bring tranquillity into internal and external worlds.

While the instructions given for this practice call for you to sit, this exercise can be carried out standing, sitting, or lying down.

You can practice the mudra and mantra separately.

1. Sit comfortably with the eyes closed or softly gazing downward. Roll the shoulders back and down.

2. Relax the elbows out to the sides, rest the forearms against the chest, and bring the hands to prayer pose slightly away from the chest. Keep the fingertips and base of the palms touching and move the fingertips slightly down so the knuckles come out toward the sides a little. Keep the fingertips touching their corresponding opposites and press the thumbs in toward the index fingers. There will be space within the hands. Looking down, the outline of the hands looks like a dove.

3. With your dove in hand, take a few gentle breaths in and out. Tune in to the energy of the dove at your hands, peace filled, gentle, evoking a sense of kindness and compassion within. Breathe in the awareness of this calm and love, breathe out anything that is not love and calm.

4. Mentally chant the mantra or, if you feel comfortable doing so, you can chant out loud, sending the vibrations into the collective field for the greater good. Inhale then chant slowly in one breath "om shanti om," the sacred sound of the universe and peace for ourselves and for all. Feel the vibration of peace on your lips and in your body.

5. Continue chanting and holding the mudra for three minutes—over time you can build to 11 minutes and even up to 30 minutes.

6. When you are ready to end, release the mudra and hands to rest. Sit quietly taking in this feeling of peace within and all around. Trust that the more you practice this mantra and mudra the more peace and compassion is created within us and in the world around us.

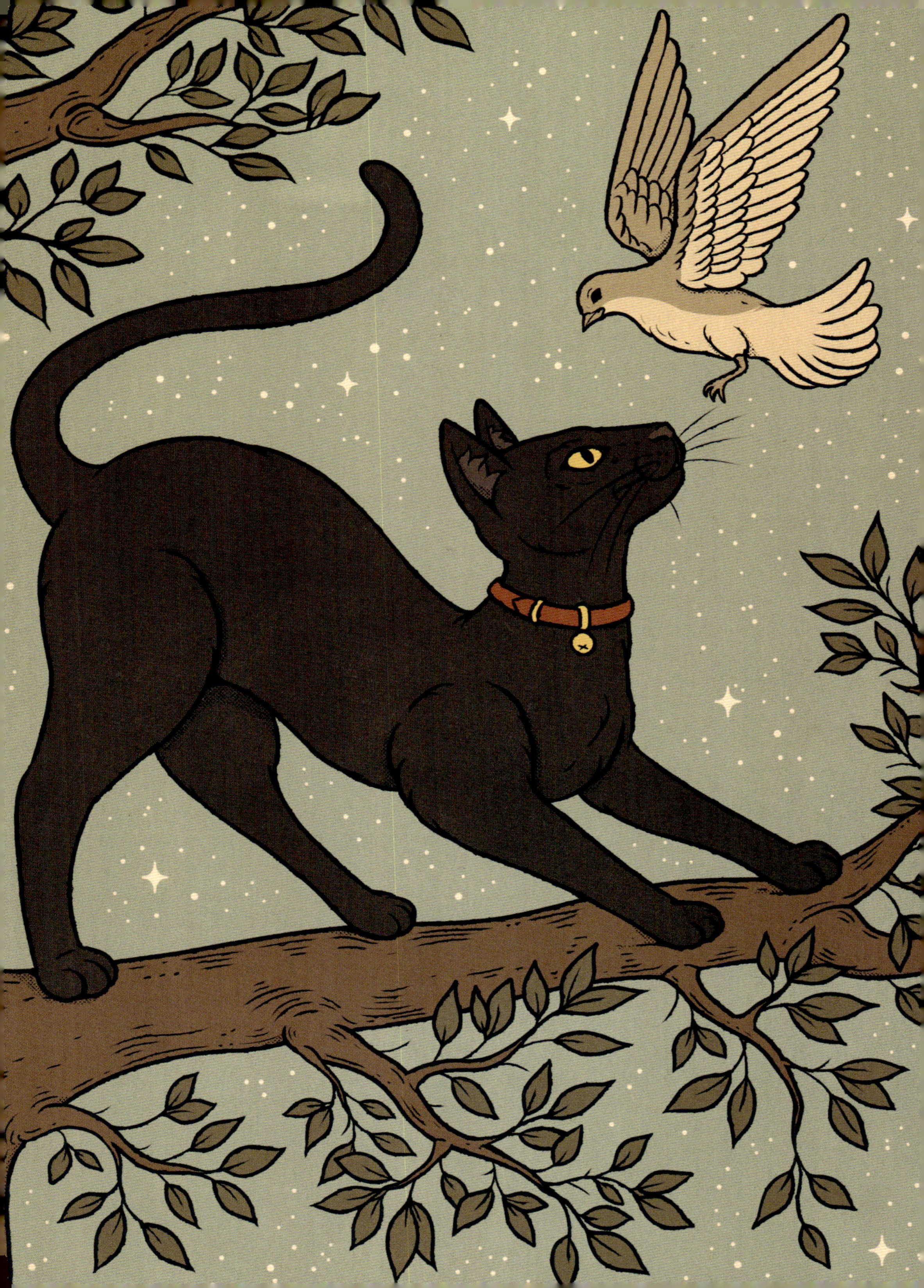

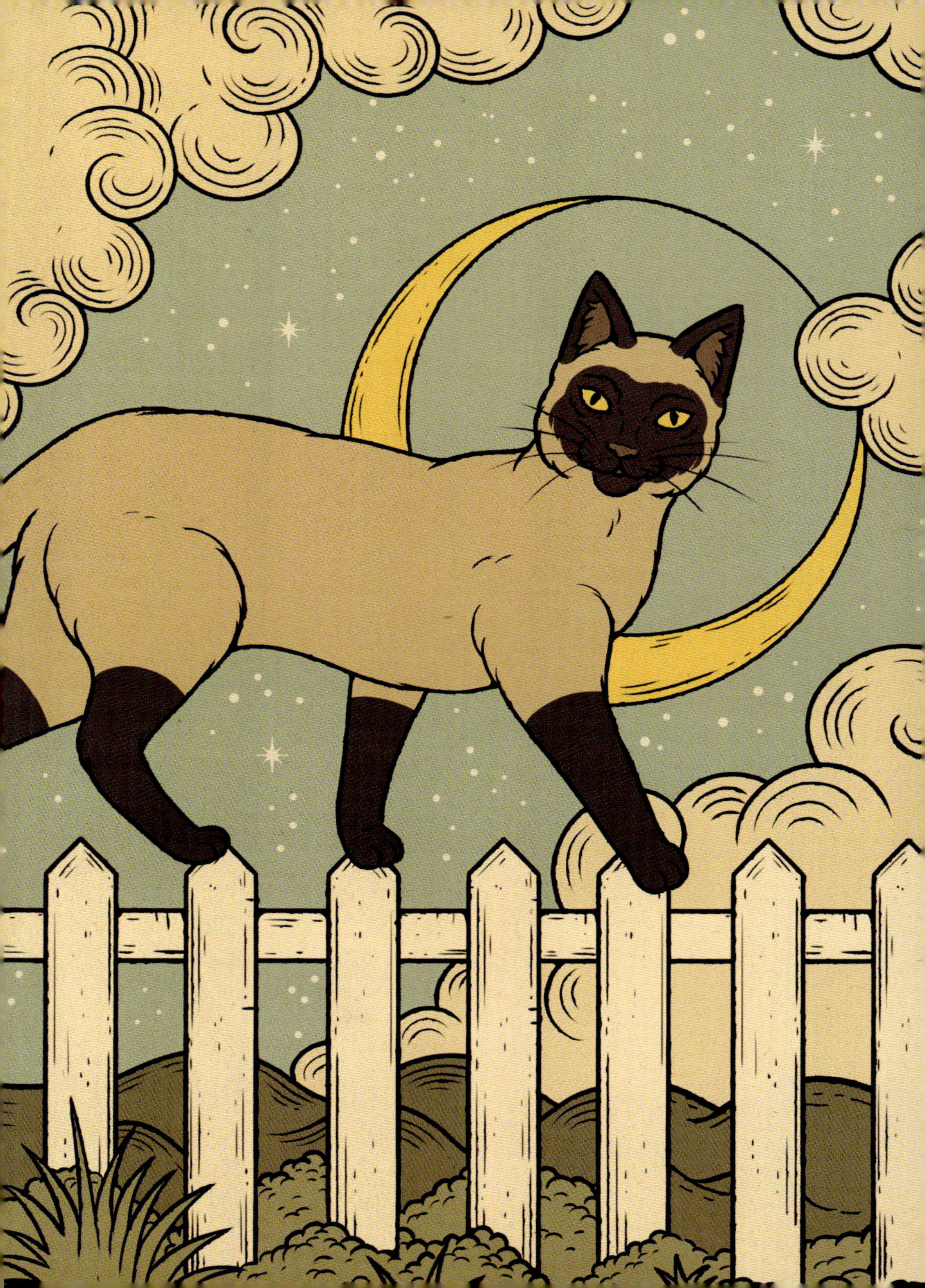

CHAPTER THREE:
JUST PLAY

Meditation doesn't always have to be practiced seated, and movement is just as important as stillness. Channel your inner playful kitten and get curious, get into a flow, and see what evolves.
In this chapter we'll explore active forms of meditation, meditative movement, yoga asanas, and energy medicine practices. Energy needs to move, and creativity opens when given the space to do so.

> "WHOEVER WANTS TO UNDERSTAND MUCH MUST PLAY MUCH."
>
> — Gottfried Benn

CAT TEACHINGS

FELINE FUN

Don't sweat the small stuff, play with it instead, says Mystic Kitty, because you'll always land on your feet!

The beauty of spending time with a kitty is that you get to play too! And the most enticing ways to play with a cat will have you thinking like a cat. Mindlessly waving that feathered bird toy on a string back and forth might be interesting the first couple of times, but that will easily bore our intelligent feline friends after a few rounds. Instead, if you ever so slowly drag that toy, as if it is a clueless prey to track and hunt, and then have it fly, you will begin to engage your cat friend and maybe have some fun yourself. Cats need playtime for their physical and mental health and—big surprise perhaps to some—humans need play too!

Play is an essential way for cats to practice and cultivate their natural hunting skills. There is a suspension of disbelief when kitty is hyper-focused, chasing and pouncing on a toy mouse on a string. That focus on the prey, and the little butt wiggle before the pounce, epitomize the cat's spirit of revelry.

We too can be encouraged to play more, and to stop taking life too seriously. By enjoying more playful activities in our lives we experience whimsy and magic, and see the wonder all around us.
To invite more levity and fun into our lives we can start with some intentional movement. If we can be light and joyful in our movement, we can bring more light and joy into our outlook on life. When we move more playfully, we enhance our intuition.

Cultivating more playfulness in life also leads to more agility, flexibility, and ability to pivot and adapt. Playfulness is key if you want to thrive, not just survive in life.

JUMPING JACKS

The caracal is a wild cat with an average weight of 18–42lb that can vault itself into the air more than ten feet to catch birds in flight. This impressive jumping cat with tufted ears can be found in Africa, the Middle East, and Turkey. The caracal's strong hind legs and agility make it an incredible jumper and hunter! Perhaps jumping more could make us humans strong and agile as well!

When was the last time you jumped up and down? Maybe when you were a kid? And more appropriately, when was the last time you just jumped up and down with joy?

Try some jumping jacks to bring a bit more joy into your life. Remember the kitten on YouTube being tickled by its owner? As it lays on its back, its paws extend out in surprise when the human tickling hand is taken away. That little kitten embodies pure joy and delight. You might also mimic that kitten as you wave your paws in the air and embody more joy by doing jumping jacks!

Jumping jacks, a full-body exercise that can improve cardiovascular health, strengthen muscles, enhance core strength and stability, and burn calories. But besides all that, they are just so much fun. We should all have more fun in life, so get jumping!

Put on an upbeat song and enjoy your jumping jacks.

1. Stand with feet roughly shoulder-width apart, arms by your sides with palms touching your thighs. Keep a slight bend in the knees with feet facing straight ahead.

2. On the inhale, jump your feet out to the sides and swing your arms out and up above your head, so your body forms a star shape.

3. On the exhale, sweep your arms back down as you jump your feet back to the starting position.

4. Repeat Steps 2–3 as many times as suits you. Five to ten repetitions might be enough to begin with. As you get fitter, you can build up to more sets of jacks.

5. For more intentional jumps, imagine that you are clearing out anything that's been heavy within you, creating space for more joy.

6. When you have completed your final set, rest the palms on the sides of the legs, close your eyes, and let your breath regulate for a minute or so. Know that you've activated the energy of joy and play in your system.

AN ADAPTATION

For a less energetic jack, instead of jumping the feet out and in, step one foot out to the side as the arms swing up, then return to the original stance. Alternate legs with each jack.

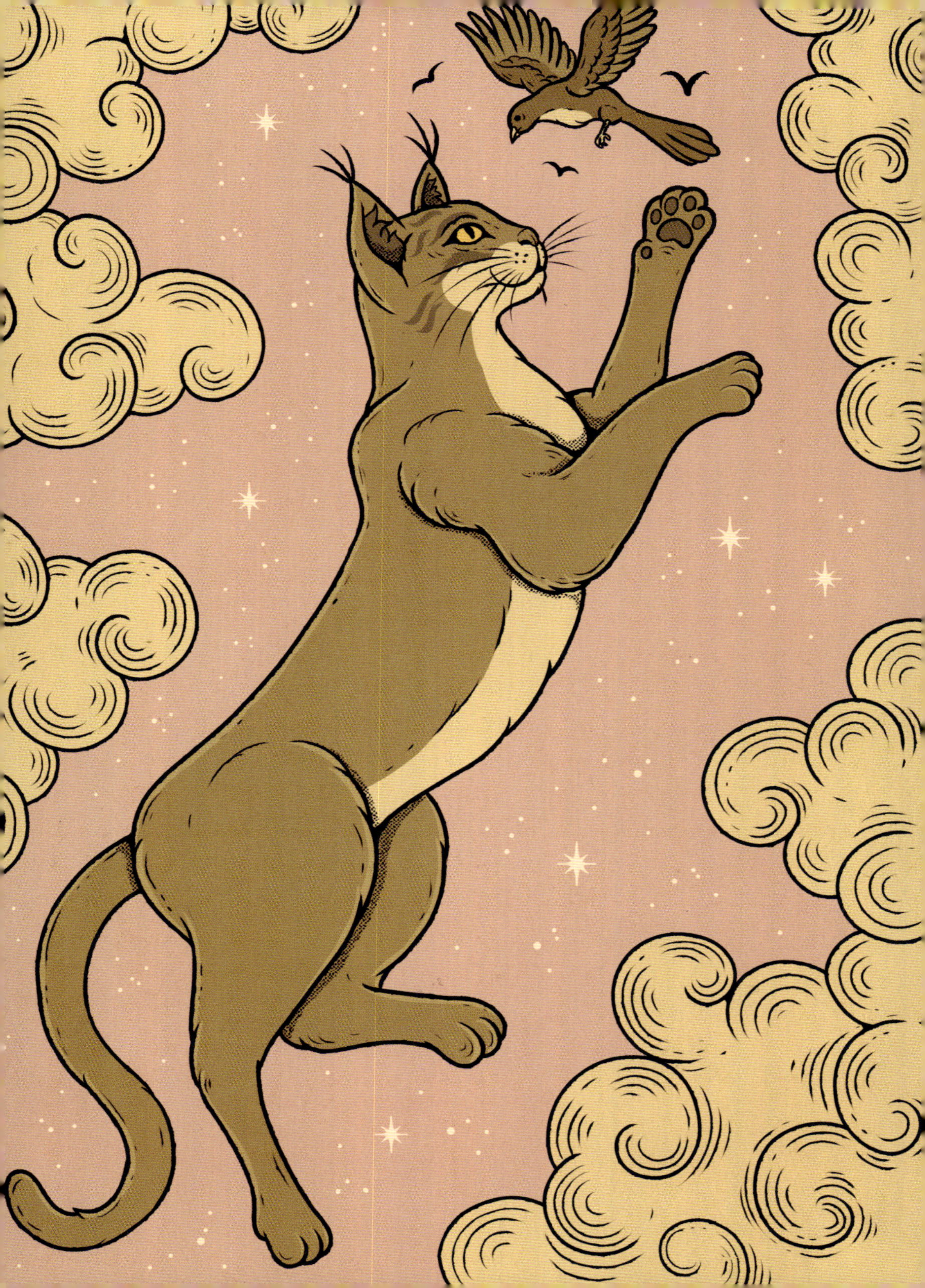

CATWALK

Cats are such elegant creatures when they walk, it's little wonder that the runway at fashion shows is known as a catwalk.

Walking one paw in front of the other is called feline direct registering, when "pawsteps" line up directly—the back paw on the same side steps right into the spot the front paw has just vacated. Cats are designed to be mini apex predators, moving in a slow and deliberate manner when stalking prey. This efficient movement helps them to be super stealthy, and reduces visible tracks. Cats also don't lift their paws up much when they walk, which minimizes noise and conserves energy.

Walking like a cat is a deeply meditative practice! It's not easy for humans to walk deliberately and elegantly, so how can we embody the lightness, focus, and agility of our kitty companions? Practice, practice, practice, and intention.

Meditative walking may seem tedious, but by moving at a snail's pace you can bring lightness, flexibility, and sure-footedness to your body, and in turn to your mind.

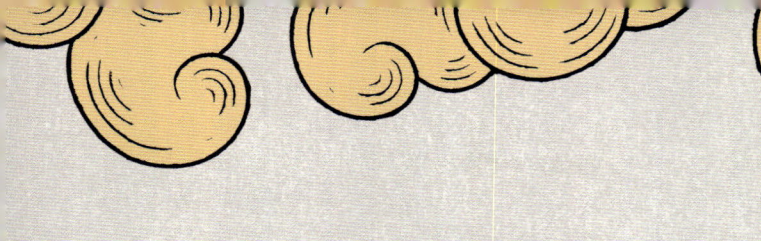

This practice involves putting one foot in front of the other with minimal lift of the foot, which is easier said than done!

Whether you are walking inside or out, make sure you have a short, clear pathway in front of you.

1. Start in a relaxed standing position with a slight bend in the knees. Keep the knees and rest of the body soft throughout the meditation. Breathe slowly.

2. Take a very slow step forward, moving like molasses as you peel the first foot off the ground from heel to toe. Keep the arms relaxed at the sides of the body.

3. Place the heel down in front of you ever so lightly, rolling the rest of the foot down slowly and surely, almost as if you were pouring sand through that foot.

4. Repeat Steps 2–3 with the other leg.

5. Continue taking slow, deliberate steps in the same way, keeping the movement soft and light, breathing slowly, and relaxing through your body.

6. As you continue walking, make sure your head is upright and gaze straight ahead. Try not to look down at your feet, but imagine yourself as a confident, elegant feline moving in a focused manner.

7. When you are ready to end, take a moment to come to a standing position with legs together and arms to the sides. Check in with your body and how you are feeling. Notice where you might feel lightness in your body, which opens space for playful flow, bringing in kitty energy.

CAT-COW ASANA

The cat-cow yoga pose combines two stretches, each one reminiscent of the animal it is named after. The benefits of this asana are, however, more cat than cow with the smooth and fluid movements of the spine.

As well as increasing the flexibility of and strengthening your spine, this dual-animal inspired movement helps to open more flow through the body. In particular, this practice balances the energy through your throat chakra—the center for accessing truth and creativity—as well as your solar plexus chakra—the center that helps you take action.

ADAPTATiONS

If you have neck issues, keep your head in a neutral position.

If you have wrist or knee injuries, you might prefer to do a seated variation and place your hands on your thighs as you arch on the inhale and round on the exhale.

A daily cat-cow practice for a few minutes is a great way to start the day, or try it any time you need a pick-me-up.

1. Position yourself on all fours on a yoga mat or cushioned surface, with extra cushioning under the knees if required. Plant your palms on the ground directly below your shoulders, and make sure your knees are directly below your hips,

2. Inhale as you lift your head, draw your face upward, stretch through your throat and neck, and arch through your lower back, pressing your stomach toward the floor. Gaze up in cow pose.

3. On the exhale, tuck your chin in toward your chest as you round through your back for cat pose. Matching breath with movement, on the inhale you bring in life-force energy to cleanse and power your system, while on the exhale you clear out and let go.

4. Repeat the sequence a few more times, moving fluidly back and forth between the poses. You might start slowly for a few rounds and then decide to speed it up, remembering to listen to your body and adjust to what it needs. It's about tuning in to what's best for your body in that moment but always matching the breath with the movement, whether fast, slow, or in-between.

5. When you have completed your preferred number of repetitions, sit back on your heels, and lower your body while spreading the knees so you can bring your head and torso as close to the ground as you can, in between the legs. Stretch the arms out straight in front of you or lay them by the side of the body with palms facing up.

6. Close your eyes and rest here for a few slow breaths. When you are ready, slowly come out of that position and notice how your body feels.

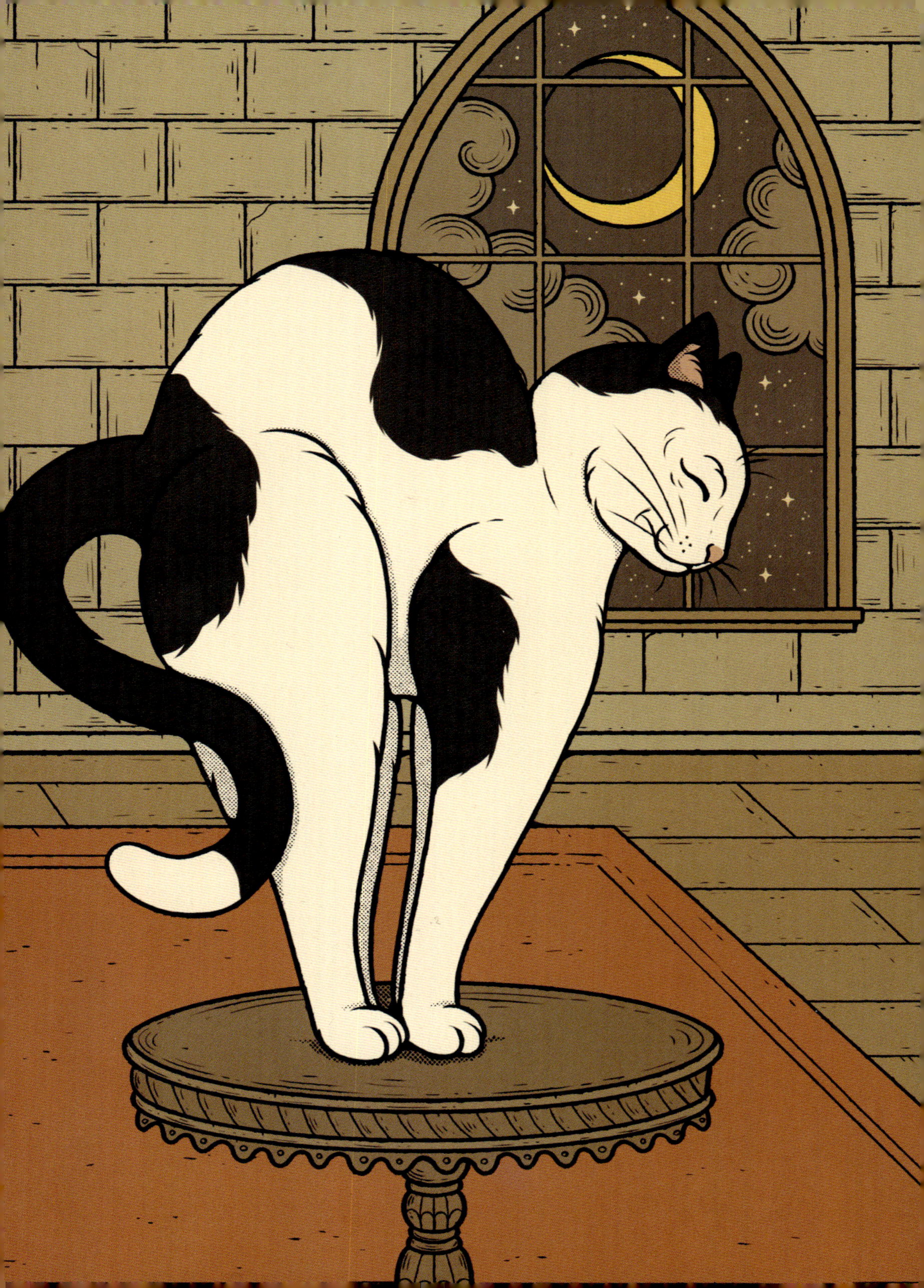

HAPPY KITTEN

Is there anything cuter than a kitten on its back, little belly exposed, reaching for its tail or hind paws, still trying to discern if these parts belong to its own body? It's a sight reminiscent of the happy baby yoga pose which we can reclaim as happy kitten pose!

There are so many benefits to lying on our backs like a happy kitten, limbs in the air and gently rocking from side to side. It's a lovely stretch and easy to accomplish; it improves hip mobility, and helps to stretch the hamstrings and strengthen the arms. The pose releases tension in the body, especially in your lower back.

In this pose you experience a sense of groundedness through your back, and when you feel grounded, supported, and calm it's easier to connect with joy and the spirit of play. In an interesting twist of balanced polarity, with your limbs in the air you'll also experience a sense of lightness and levity.

This pose is deeply relaxing and restorative, and a great way to play and self-soothe. You can also extend it into a mini asana.

1. Lie flat on your back on a mat or the floor, feeling the support underneath you through your entire body. Take a gentle breath in through your nose and out.

2. Hug your knees in toward your chest. Bend your knees as close as you can to a 90-degree angle so that the soles of your feet turn up toward the ceiling.

3. Reach forward with your hands and hold your feet, either on the inside or outside.

4. Open and spread your knees, letting them drop toward your armpits.

5. From here, flex your heels while still holding on with your hands and gently rock from side to side. Take a few gentle breaths here and feel your body relaxing into the pose.

6. You might want to hold for five slow breaths or as long as it feels good. When you are ready to end, simply release the hands from the feet and lower the feet and arms down to the mat.

ADAPTATIONS

You may find it more comfortable to hold the shins or ankles.

If you have knee injuries, hold behind the thighs.

KITTY ASANA

If you want to turn this into a mini, kitty-inspired asana sequence, continue into the next pose.

1. From the happy kitty pose, come into a lazy kitty stretch by first lowering the legs to the ground, lying flat.

2. Pull the right knee up toward your chest. Take your left hand to the right knee and pull the knee down toward the ground on the left side, twisting across the body.

3. Open through the chest and extend the right arm straight out to the side along the ground, turning your head to the right and gazing at the right palm. Hold for three to five breaths.

4. Release the twist and return to lying flat on the ground, arms by your sides, head back to center.

5. Repeat Steps 2–3, pulling the left knee in and down to the right side, with the left arm extended to the left with palm up.

6. Release the twist and return to lying flat on the ground, arms by your sides, head back to center.

KITTY CURL AND ARCH

If you've seen photos on the internet of kittens squeezed into the comfort of a glass bowl, it's easy to imagine that cats are indeed liquid. That's not too far from the truth, since cats are wondrously fluid and agile, in part due to their mastery of stretching.

Cats stretch often, an inadvertently regular program that keeps them supple. A classic cat stretch, often made upon waking, sees paws pushed forward, body arched, and backside up in the air, and is a stretch that serves to wake up the muscles ready to jump into action.

This type of stretching is known as pandiculation, an involuntary contraction, release, and lengthening of the muscles that is quite different from voluntary stretching. It's also known as a full-body yawn, and is a natural way of releasing stress and resetting the body. The more you can pandiculate after a cat nap, or anytime you've been sedentary for a while, the more relaxed you might be!

Yawning itself is pandiculation, and to induce a gloriously satisfying full-body yawn, begin by noticing that just by reading the word "yawn" you want to yawn. Let that yawn happen, feeling the contraction of muscles in your face, bring your arms up over your head to contract slightly, and lead into a natural extension stretch.

Pandiculation gives your brain the feedback to release tension in the body. The contraction is a pleasurable sensation in the same way a yawn is pleasurable. It lights up your brain through your sensory motor system, and through the slowness of opening and lengthening, the brain can begin to make changes to release.

We can direct our awareness and be present in the internal experience of opening and letting go through a process of contraction and slow release. Let's value our internal experience, connect back to sensing and being in our bodies. Slow motion and less effort give us more benefits.

Just as the cat eases itself into action after a period of rest, so must we. Perform this seated stretch whenever you need a break from a sedentary position. Move slowly and intentionally through this sequence, contracting the muscles and then slowly releasing so that the muscles and brain can be triggered and activated, inducing pandiculation.

1 From a seated position, let your arms drop to the sides of your body.

2 Inhale as you slowly squeeze and lift your shoulders toward your ears into a contraction and a deliciously tight squeeze.

3 On the exhale, slowly and gently roll the shoulders back and down, feeling the shoulder blades move together and the chest open. Relax.

4 Rest for another slow breath in and out.

5 Repeat Steps 2–4 a few more times, matching breath with slow movement. Bringing your awareness inside, imagine feeling the contraction and slow lengthening from the inside.

DANCE & SHAKE

In the musical Cats, *based on T.S. Eliot's* Old Possum's Book of Practical Cats, *the cats gather for the Jellicle Ball, where they perform to see who might be chosen to be reborn into a new life. We might take this as a kitty instructive: dance, shake, and move to reset and revitalize.*

Animals in the wild shake to release stress and tension after a life-threatening encounter. By shaking, they release adrenalin and cortisol so that they can regulate their system and go about the rest of their day—even though just moments before they had been frantically running at speed to escape a predator. This shaking is called a tremor mechanism, and it is nature's way of helping all animals to clear out trauma. It's a natural reflex mechanism that begins in the limbic brain, which is involved in emotional responses. The shaking and vibrating helps restore homeostasis to the system.

Imagine yourself reborn, free of what's been holding you back. Try dancing and shaking in the spirit of integrating what's worth keeping and then clearing emotional and energetic clutter.

Incorporate this practice into your daily routine as a way of resetting your body.

1. Choose a song that feels uplifting and gets you moving. You'll be playing music later in the practice.

2. Standing still to begin with, take a gentle breath in and out and bring your awareness inward. Notice how and what you are feeling and sensing. Notice any areas of tension or discomfort as you scan through your body.

3. With knees soft and slightly bent, gently bounce through the legs for about a minute.

4. Let the arms hang as you allow the bouncing to move into the rest of the body. Tune into your body and let it direct the shaking. Maybe the shoulders want to shake out, or the hands and feet want to clear things out. Ask your body and feel into what it wants to shake and move.

5. Keep the breath steady as the body and its various parts continue to shake. Allow your body to move the way it wants, listening in as you follow the natural inclination of your body to flow.

6. Continue shaking for a few minutes. Observe any emotions, thoughts, and sensations that arise as you move. Observe without judgment. Think that as you shake, anything that is stagnant and stuck gets to move. Feel that the shaking clears your mind, body, and field of energy.

7. Now turn on your music and continue to shake and dance. Let your body direct the movement and feel into the joy of the music. Think that as you move and clear, you are now activating the essence of play and creative flow in your body and system.

8. When you are ready to finish, you will feel a natural slowing, a gradual stillness as the music ends. Use this time to take in the stillness of your body as it comes to standing rest and integration. Notice how you are feeling.

LION'S BREATH

Lions have the loudest roar of all the big cats, and yet our mini house lions do not. What gives? It essentially comes down to a piece of cartilage. Roar or purr, because you can't have both.

Big cats have a full-throated, loud roar because of a piece of cartilage that gives the larynx extra flexibility to reverberate a roar so loud it can be felt miles away.

How might you take your space and establish strong, clear boundaries in all aspects of your life, like the king of the jungle does? Own your power while retaining that playful cat energy with a yogic breathing practice called lion's breath.

When we learn to roar like a lion, we activate and strengthen our throat chakra, which supports our creative expression. Lion's breath—or lion's pose—is a great practice for clearing stress and tension as you stretch the muscles in your face and neck. It strengthens your lungs and vocal cords, and can relieve anxiety and fear, making you more confident, lion-hearted, and lighthearted.

The "ha" sound made in lion's breath represents the energy of the sun, so this is considered a warming breath and practice. Sticking your tongue out in lion's breath might also increase your ability to be self-assured, silly, and spirited: in other words, essential cat energy!

Practice lion's breath daily, throughout the day, or anytime you feel sluggish and slow. Test out this practice in place of caffeine and a sugary pick-me-up. Set an intention before beginning the practice to help you show up more fully in your life.

1. Take some time to set your intention. Think of the ways in which you would like this lion's breath to support you, perhaps helping you feel more confident and empowered, whatever feels best.

2. Sit on a chair or on your heels on a yoga mat, with your knees together. Whichever position you choose, make sure your spine is long and tall. Close your eyes, rest your hands on your thighs, and let your breath be long and even.

3. Roll your shoulders backward and allow the shoulder blades to relax down your back. Continue to slow and deepen your breath.

4. Inhale through your nose, then open your mouth wide, ready to exhale. Stick out your tongue and make a drawn-out sound of "ha" with the exhale. Picture the sun energy of the sound, and use that to clear what might be holding you back on the conscious and unconscious levels. Clear whatever has been keeping you from playing, and step more fully into your big-cat energy.

5. Repeat Step 4, making the inhalations and exhalations equal in length, while also slowing and deepening the breath.

6. Practice for three to five rounds to begin with. With more practice, you can build to ten rounds.

7. To end, bring your tongue back in, close your mouth, and allow your face to relax, breathing naturally in and out through your nose.

8. Rest and relax into the lion energy that you've harnessed, establishing clear boundaries in your life, and activating courage to be your authentic self, living your truth and leading with integrity. Close with gratitude.

BLOWING OUT THE VENOM BREATH

Some feline behaviorists believe that cats learned to hiss from snakes! Does that seem far-fetched, but also not at all? Mimicry, or imitation, happens throughout nature, so it needn't be entirely dismissed. A snake's hiss is feared, so some believe that early cat ancestors learned to mimic the hissing sound as a defense mechanism, a warning to others to back off.

Snakes, cats, and geese all hiss in warning, and in fear. We human animals might also jump on the hissing bandwagon, with a practice that releases fear and anger.

Blowing out the venom is the name given to an exercise from Eden Energy Medicine that helps to clear emotional "venom," such as toxic thoughts, stress, and tension. It's an excellent practice for overwhelm as well.

Pent-up emotions and stress act like poisons in our systems. Just as the liver and gallbladder work to rid our bodies of physical poisons, so this practice, using the Traditional Chinese Medicine "shhhhhh" sound, helps to restore balance to the energetic liver and gallbladder systems. An unbalanced liver is associated with frustration, anger, jealousy, resentment, and guilt.

Use this practice to balance energy and clear out emotional venom and toxic thoughts and feelings.

1. Stand with your hands resting on your thighs with fingers spread out. Take a few gentle breaths, allowing the exhale to be longer than the inhale. Feel into the support of the ground beneath you, and imagine connecting to earth energy.

2. On the inhale, sweep your arms out to the sides and above your head, gathering the hands into fists overhead. Imagine gathering everything and anything that you'd like to release, such as anger, anxiety, fear, frustration, discomfort, or any emotion you'd like to clear out.

3. Think about the specific emotion or situation as being within your fists, then sweep your arms down and throw what is held there down to the ground, opening your fists as you release it. Make a loud "shhhhhh" sound as the arms lower, while throwing away the "venom."

4. Repeat Steps 2–3 until the practice feels complete.

5. Finish by drawing the arms up one last time, except this time gather strength into your hands as you inhale.

6. Draw that strength into your heart space with the "shhhhhh" sound, bringing one hand over the other at the center of the chest. Breathe long and slow and receive and activate that strength throughout your entire body.

BLOWING OUT THE VENOM BREATH

TIGER POSE

Little cats possess big-cat energy, and they do not shy away from getting their needs met. We can also incorporate more big-cat energy into our own lives by drawing clear boundaries and being vocal about our needs, but in order to do so we need a stable foundation.

In Tai Chi, the tiger represents power, courage, and success. When we mimic tiger movements we can increase our vitality and bolster our health. We can move stagnant energy, remove toxins from the body, and balance our physical and subtle energetic bodies through these movements.

Tiger balancing on front paws is a seemingly simple yet deeply strengthening pose. What happens in the physical also happens in the emotional and energetic layers of our being, so when we can be intentional in strengthening our core and stabilizing our balance, we can also be more balanced in our lives.

Ground into a stable place physically and energetically with this exercise.

1. Stand with the legs about hip-width apart with your hands on your hips. Slowly shift your body weight from side to side a few times.

2. Keeping your weight on your left leg, lift the right knee up to 90 degrees. Reach the arms forward and up with elbows bent and slightly out to the sides. Face the palms out to the front and curl the fingers to make tiger claws.

3. Balance here as you breathe, stabilizing your core. Lengthen through the spine, looking straight ahead and breathing into your center of gravity. Breathe into your lower dantian (a few fingers below your navel) which is your energy center, the storehouse of your vital energy and power.

4. Hold the pose for up to 30 seconds.

5. Return the right leg to the ground and bring the arms down. Place your hands back on your hips, and again slowly shift your body weight from side to side.

6. Repeat Steps 2–4 with the left leg lifted.

7. Lower the leg and return to your original position.

8. Place one hand over the other at your lower dantian. With eyes closed, connect your breath to this place of personal power and essence. When that feels complete, release the hands and open your eyes.

AN ADAPTATiON

To embrace the spirit of play, at the end of Step 5 you can turn your hands into paws and claws, do a little tiger scratch, and add a roar or two from your lower belly.

TIGER POSE

PAW TAPS FOR FUNSIES

Cats love to sit innocently on a table or counter and, with one little paw, start tap-tap-tapping an object until they knock it off the edge. It's certainly a special and innate cat skill. Luckily for us, we can also tap for more fun in our lives.

The less fear we have in our systems, the more fun we can have in our lives!

In Traditional Chinese Medicine there are invisible energy pathways running throughout the body called meridians. We can work with these meridians through acupuncture, acupressure, and tapping to balance and strengthen energy in our system.

Tap the kidney meridian to balance fear and strengthen courage which in turn will allow you to have more fun.

This practice can be carried out lying down, sitting, or even walking. Practice any time you are feeling fearful or just want to have more fun!

1. Use both hands to locate your collarbone. Find the two nubby protrusions along the collarbone on either side at the notch of your sternum. You have a choice now:

   - Use your fingers to massage the area right under the protrusions.
   - Lightly tap the area with the fingers.
   - Make fists and thump in that area.

2. As you massage, tap, or thump this area related to one of the kidney meridian points, inhale through the nose and exhale through the mouth. Keep this breath going as you continue to tap.

3. With your eyes closed or gazing softly, imagine that you are working through any fear and creating more space for courage and joy in your body, in your energy field, and in your life. Continue for three minutes.

4. When you are ready to end, simply release the hands to rest and breathe slowly and easily through the nose.

JUST PLAY

LISTEN UP, PUSSYCATS

Cats have excellent hearing, with ranges about three times higher than humans. They have 32 muscles in their outer ears to help them pinpoint sounds. Maybe being able to hear more and able to pinpoint sounds helps them to be more at ease in the world, and being more at ease in the world allows them to be more playful.

This is a super simple practice from applied kinesiology that helps us release stress and take in more information by stimulating the vagus nerve. The vagus nerve is one of the longest nerves in the in the parasympathetic nervous system and controls many functions such as digestion, heart rate, and breathing. With the auricular ear release, we are stimulating the vagus nerve to rest and digest, allowing us to take in our environment calmly and invite more joy into our lives.

This practice can be carried out lying down, sitting, or even walking.

1. With both hands, massage and gently rub and pull both ears all over at the same time. Do this for a minute or so in a way that feels good for you. This should not feel painful.

2. When you are ready to end, release the hands and just notice if you are feeling more calm yet energized. Now, go and have some fun!

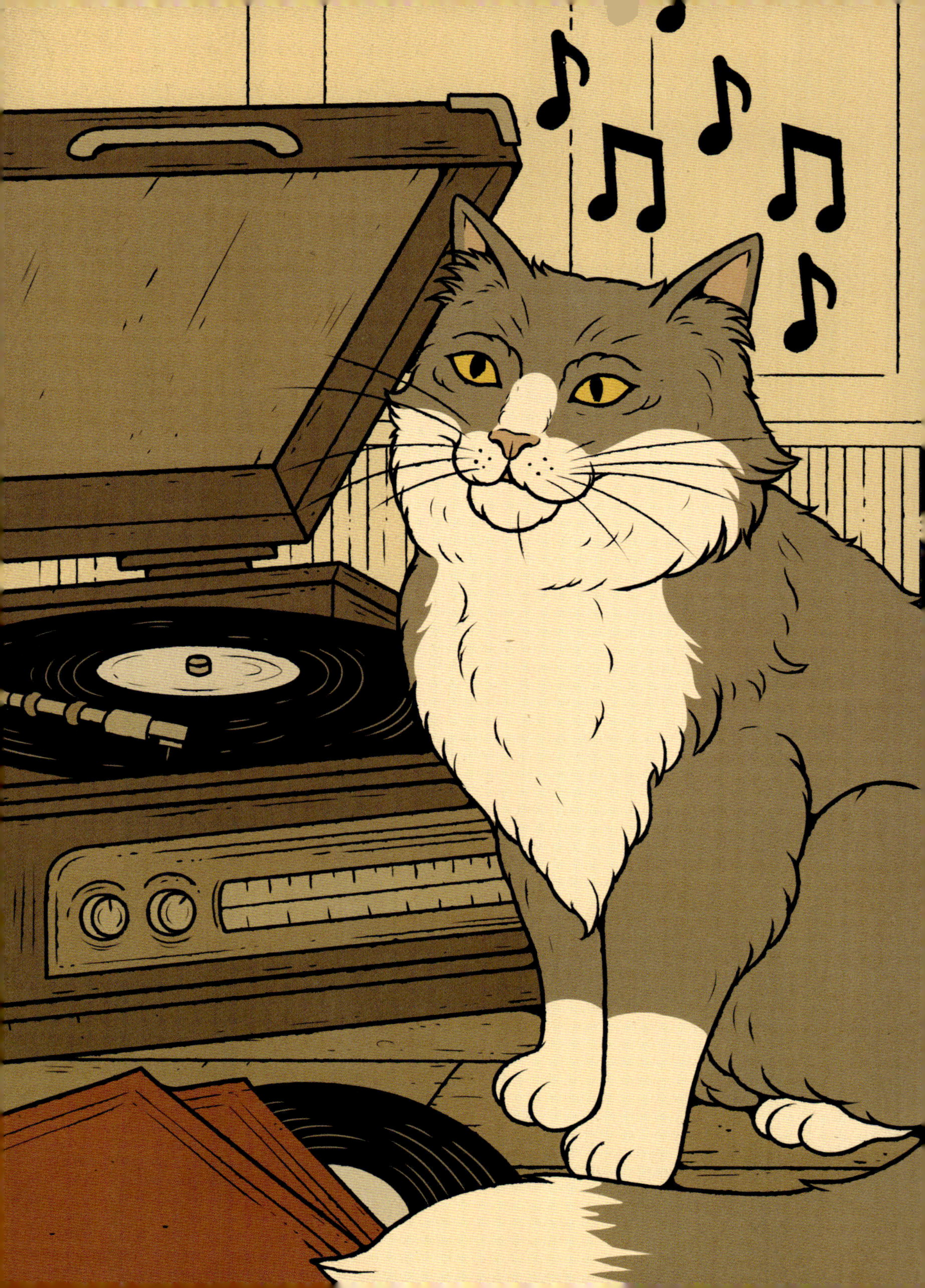

CHAPTER FOUR

JUST REST

Cats are excellent sleepers. Deep rest is best, say all cats, great and small. It's time for us, too, to come into stillness. In this chapter we'll explore different ways to strengthen the parasympathetic nervous system to properly rest and digest, and learn meditations and simple somatic practices to release stress and ground energy for nourishing, nurturing sleep.

> **"TAKE REST; A FIELD THAT HAS RESTED GIVES A BOUNTIFUL CROP."**
>
> – OVID

CAT TEACHINGS

CATNAPS

Nowadays we are all more aware of the importance of good-quality sleep for our health and wellbeing, since rest regulates and resets the body. Poor sleep, of course, makes us tired, but the long-term cumulative effects of inadequate sleep are harmful for our health.

Felines are the masters of rest, with lions sleeping for 20 hours a day, while our smaller feline companions sleep between 12 to 18 hours a day.

Cats big and small sleep in what is known as a polyphasic pattern, meaning they have multiple periods of sleep throughout the day. This ability to nap helps wild cats conserve their energy for the hunt, whereas house cats have kept this instinct despite the fact that they no longer rely on the hunt for food since they have trained their humans to wait on them hand and paw! House cats take opportunistic catnaps throughout the day and sleep for longer periods as well.

Cats sleep in a variety of positions, from imitating a loaf of bread or contorting into a pretzel shape to spreading out in the middle of a surface or perched on an edge. As if anyone needed more proof that felines are perfection, cats often sleep curled up in a tight round shape, giving us a Fibonacci spiral, the golden ratio, considered to indicate the sacred geometry of life, the natural order, and the balance, beauty, and harmony of the universe.

There are a number of practices we can tap into to encourage a short, refreshing sleep, or to prepare for better sleep each night. Our feline friends have been giving us a masterclass in rest, are you taking notes?

BOX BREATHING

What do cats, quantum theory, and Navy SEALs have in common? The answer is "a box."

Schrödinger's cat-in-a-box thought experiment demonstrates the quantum physics principle that particles can be in multiple states at the same time, until they are observed—and then the box is opened.

Cats big and small love a box. Studies have found that when cats in shelters have boxes to hide in, they are less stressed. Instinctively, cats will curl into a snug box where they feel warm and safe.

The element of a box is also an important component of a breath practice that Navy SEALs swear by. It's aptly named box breathing, or *sama vritti pranayama*, which in Sanskrit means "same/equal wave," and involves performing each stage of the practice for a specified number of counts. It's an incredible breath practice combined with visualization of a square that helps you to calm yourself and achieve a relaxed focus.

Also known as square breathing, this is a wonderful pranayama for before bed to encourage deeper rest. You can also use it at any time to ground anxiety and stress or when you need some calm, focused energy.

⚠️

This breath retention practice is contraindicated for those who have heart issues, blood pressure issues or are pregnant. Simply inhale and exhale instead of holding breath in or out

This breath practice, in and out through the nose, is divided into four equal parts of: inhale/hold/exhale/hold. It is usually practiced to counts of four, although you can decide on a suitable count, so if that feels too long you can choose a shorter count for each inhale/hold/exhale/hold.

1 Lie down or sit in a chair and take a few slow breaths in and out through the nose before starting the box-breath pattern. Close your eyes and notice how you are feeling.

2 Breathing through the nose, the pattern of box breathing looks like this:

- Inhale for a count of four.
- Hold for a count of four.
- Exhale for a count of four.
- At the end of the exhale, hold the breath out for a count of four.

3 Once you've had a chance to practice and get to grips with the breathing sequence, you can add visualization.

- On the inhale, imagine drawing one side of a square in your mind's eye.
- On the hold, visualize drawing the second side of the square.
- On the exhale, draw the third line of the square.
- On the final hold, draw the fourth side of the square in your mind's eye.

4 Complete a few repetitions of a full set. You should find the breath and visualization combination to be deeply calming. If you feel anxious or the breath is strained, use a shorter count.

5 When you are ready to end, finish the set and allow the breath to return to its natural flow as you tune in to the stable symbol of a square, feeling relaxed and focused.

BOX BREATHING

SOMATIC EYE PRESS

There might be nothing sweeter than the sight of a sleeping cat with its paws covering its eyes. This evolutionary behavior most likely comes from a need to protect the eyes and keep the face warm while sleeping. And that's our cue for this next somatic breath practice.

Somatic therapies and practices are in their heyday, and rightfully so; it's a long-overdue frontier of medicine that is gaining some ground.

It is thought that the body holds unexpressed trauma and emotions which can manifest as physical issues, and a professional somatic facilitator can guide you on the deep work to release what's being held in the body. In somatic modalities, we say "the issue is in the tissues."

To explore what we may have pushed down deep into our bodies years ago takes a level of commitment. However, there are also ways you can practice somatic movement at home to help create more safety in your nervous system in order to deeply rest.

In this practice we will work with the eyes, which are connected to the nervous system through the retina, optic nerve, and cranial nerves. The health of your nervous system is connected to your eyes, so the ease in your nervous system might be reflected by the vitality of your eyes. There is a constant stream of information through your eyes, whether open or closed, so it's important to help relax them with intentionality.

Practice at least once a day to see what shifts in your body and in your life.

1. Sit upright with enough cushions on your lap to comfortably rest your elbows, or sit at a table covered with material to cushion your elbows.

2. Rest your elbows on the cushioning and bring the heels of your palms and wrists to lightly press into your eyes as you close them. Allow your head and eyes to sink into your hands.

3. Let your arms and elbows sink into the cushioned support. Softening through the shoulder, let everything sink down and in.

4. Breathing long and slow, continue pressing gently. Tune in to your eyes, feeling the light pressure and warmth there.

5. Give appreciation for your eyes, these beautiful, incredible parts of ourselves, open to your felt-sense awareness. Continue lightly pressing and breathing and visualize each retina connecting to the optic nerve. The optic nerves run straight from the eyes to the back of the head, to the visual cortex, helping you to process what you see. Imagine that just considering the eyes, retina, and optic nerve can light up those parts, then allow them to rest.

6. Consider that by relaxing your eyes you can relax your brain. Actively relaxing the eyes further helps the nervous system to rest. By breathing and making contact with the eyes in this way, we can begin to restore balance to our nervous system.

7. Continue for a few minutes and when you are ready to end, slide the palms down along the face, until the fingers are over the eyes, slightly spaced apart. Even with the eyes closed, light can still get through the open fingers. Take a little time to acclimatize here, then let the hands come to rest on your lap, eyes still closed.

8. When you are ready, very slowly flutter the eyes open to adjust your vision.

SOMATIC EYE PRESS

LUNAR BREATH

Cats have long been associated with the moon, and the mysterious feline contemplating the mysteries of the moon is a familiar illustrative trope.

The ancient Egyptian goddess of the moon, Bast, has the head of a cat, and in storytelling cats are often the companions of night-flying witches, their familiars. There's a supposed provincial Chinese legend that white cats go onto the rooftops to steal moonbeams. Is it so wrong to want to capture a moonbeam for oneself?

In yogic traditions, the energy pathway through the right nostril is related to the sun and on the left nostril to the moon. Sun energy is considered masculine and the energy of action. Moon energy is said to be feminine, intuitive, and receptive. Moon energy is calming and is related to emotions, introspection, intuition, and dreams.

Chandra nadi pranayama is a lunar energy pathway breath practice that we can use to harness the power of the moon to calm ourselves, while also learning more about ourselves. Think of it as catching moonbeams to illuminate your inner world.

This is a simple pranayama that can regulate our system so that we can begin to gather insight and reflect the best versions of ourselves out into the world. You might work with this breath to help bring clarity to an issue. Here's to illuminating the mysteries in the dark, honing vision, and receiving insight. We should all be more like white cats gathering moonbeams!

This is a great calming practice for before bed, if you wake in the night with racing thoughts, or any time you need to tap into the wisdom of the moon and quell anxiety.

1. Practice daily for a week or more and notice what becomes clearer.

2. Sit upright or lie down in a comfortable position.

3. Inhale fully through your nose and release the exhale slowly through your nose. Close your eyes or soften your gaze.

4. With the left hand, bring the thumb and index finger to touch in gyan mudra (see page 118), to receive wisdom and insight. Rest the hand in your lap or, if you are lying down, rest your arm on the side of the body with the mudra facing upward.

5 Raise the right index finger and curl the rest of the fingers into the palm, with the thumb wrapped over the top. Gently hold down the right nostril with the right index finger.

6 Breathe slowly in and out through the left nostril. Each breath in and out is relaxing your system, and so opening you to insight. Imagine breathing in lunar energy, with each breath strengthening your intuition and illuminating what has been in the dark.

7 Continue in the same way, slowing the inhale and exhale through the left nostril. Practice for a minimum of three minutes to begin with to calm your system. Over time you can build up to 11 minutes for even more benefits.

8 When you are ready to end, gently remove the right index finger from the right nostril and breathe normally. Take a moment to sit quietly, trusting that your system is receiving all that it needs. Give gratitude to the moon.

PAWS OUT

Sometimes cats rest or sleep with their paws stretched out, often as a way to regulate temperature. With their paws extended they can also quickly spring into action from rest, if they need to.

We can adopt this position ourselves to regulate our system to support a good night's sleep. The position we will adapt is called paschimottanasana, or seated forward bend pose. Forward bends trigger the parasympathetic nervous system to help us rest and digest, since when we fold forward, the vagus nerve is stimulated through the stretching of the abdominal area and the head and neck.

Seated forward bend is a deeply restorative and rejuvenating pose that can help to ease stress and boost wellbeing. You'll also be stretching the hamstrings and lower back, and massaging internal organs.

⚠️ This pose is not recommended for those who are pregnant or who have back or neck pain, sciatica, a slipped disc, a hernia, glaucoma, or high blood pressure.

Seated forward bend can be practiced at any time, but when practiced at night it can relieve tension and release stress from the day, better preparing mind and body for deep rest.

Practice on a yoga mat on the ground.

1. Sit upright with the legs extended, keeping a slight bend in the knees.

2. Inhale deeply as you lengthen through the spine, sitting up tall.

3. Exhale twice as long as you stretch your body forward, hinging from the hips with the arms extended. If you can, wrap the index and middle fingers and thumbs around the big toes You should be able to relax into this pose, so do not force it. See Adaptations, below right, if needed.

4. Allow the head and chest to rest on the legs if possible; if not, allow them to hang (see also Adaptations, right). Keep the back straight and do not be tempted to round it in order to get your head onto your legs. Make sure the knees are not locked, but maintain a slight bend.

5. Relax into the pose. Breathing slowly and deeply, see if you can stretch a little bit more, without straining yourself—even if it's just for a few seconds. With time, you will strengthen the lower back so you are able to fully lengthen into this pose.

6. Breathe slow and easy while resting in this pose for as long as you can comfortably maintain it.

7. When you are ready to end, slowly make your way up to an upright, seated position with arms at your sides.

ADAPTATIONS

You can modify Step 3 by holding the thighs, knees, calves, or sides of the feet as you bend forward. Choose whatever is comfortable.

You might like to position a bolster cushion on your legs to rest the head and chest on.

Position a rolled-up towel under the knees if you require some support there.

SLOW BLINKS

When your cat slow blinks it is likely a sign that they feel comfortable and safe, and perhaps even that they love you. The love we feel for our animal companions in return is unconditional. What if we could somehow learn to love ourselves unconditionally?

In hypnosis we use slow blinks as a way of bringing a client into a trance. This is known as fractionation, where a client can be guided slowly and surely into a deeper state of relaxation. We can also use it for self-hypnosis, which is especially potent before bed to guide the subconscious mind into sleep with more love and kindness. In short, we can slow blink our way into more love, trust, and affection for ourselves. This is a potent tool to help you reset and focus on what you actually want in life.

Let's slow blink our way to a regulated nervous-system, self-love, and compassion before bed. And if you happen to sleep deeply through the night, you will wake up at your usual time feeling rested and revitalized.

1. Whether lying in bed or sitting comfortably, place one hand at the center of your chest and the other on the solar plexus or belly. Set an intention for how it might feel to send love and compassion to yourself. If that feels difficult to access, imagine a kitty you have loved unconditionally alongside a version of yourself as a young child, with the two of them becoming the object of your love. If you have another intention you want to work with, tune in to a feeling that you would like to embody more of in your life; it can even be as simple as an intention to sleep more soundly and deeply.

2. Pick a spot slightly above your line of vision that you can gaze at comfortably, for example a point directly in front of you where the wall meets the ceiling.

3. Slowly blink your eyes as you count:

- One—open and close the eyes.
- Two—open and close the eyes.
- Three—open and close the eyes . . .
- . . . and so on until your eyes start to feel heavy with each slow blink.

4. At some point you should feel your eyelids so heavy that you'll want to close them and rest in that comfort of heaviness.

5. With the eyes resting comfortably closed, imagine a soft golden light, as the energy of self-love, gently moving up through the body from the soles of the feet to the crown of the head, where it pours out and all around you like a fountain, then circles back to the feet where the cycle continues.

6. Once you've completed a few rounds of this visualization—perhaps three to start with—reverse the direction and see the light moving from the crown down through the body, out at the soles of the feet where the energy then moves up and around the body and back into the head.

7. When you have completed a few cleansing rounds of running the energy in both directions, imagine that your intention is placed in this light as it pours in and out, infusing your body and field with the light of your intention. Three rounds in each direction is a good starting practice.

8. When you are ready to end, tell yourself that you are ready to come back and count:

- Three—bring your awareness back into this space.
- Two—feel your body being supported.
- One—open your eyes and feel wonderful.

PROGRESSIVE RELAXATION

Studies have shown that watching humorous videos can be good for your health, since laughter supports your immune system, lowers stress hormones, and increases endorphin production in the brain. Watching funny cat videos after a long, tough day at work might just be what the feline physician prescribes!

When we laugh we tense our facial and core muscles, and a hearty laugh can actually work all the muscles in the body. Perhaps you can plan to get in some kitty comedy videos and log those cat-inspired laughs each day.

While we don't want to engage in screen hilarity too close to bedtime, we can take a cue from the idea of squeezing the muscles during laughter in a practice that can help the body to relax into sleep. It's called progressive muscle relaxation and it's an easy technique to incorporate while in bed.

In this practice you will systematically squeeze and release the muscles while adding a mindful breath to the process to deepen your awareness and start to strengthen interoception—the ability to notice what's going on inside the body.

As well as at bedtime, this practice can work wonders if you are up in the middle of the night and want to get back to sleep.

You will start this technique from the bottom and move upward through the body.

1. Lie down with arms out to the sides and palms facing up. Inhale through the nose and exhale more slowly out through the nose.

2. Bring your awareness to your feet. Inhale first, then tense and arch the feet. Hold the breath for four seconds as you squeeze. Gently exhale for eight seconds as you slowly release and relax the muscles. Feel the feet almost sinking into the surface beneath you.

3. Repeat Step 2, working progressively up through the body, tensing with the inhalation and releasing with the exhalation. Work through these areas of the body:

- Calves
- Thighs
- Buttocks/hips
- Belly/lower back
- Diaphragm
- Rib cage
- Chest
- Hands
- Arms
- Shoulders/neck
- Face

If you aren't able to fully feel yourself tensing a certain muscle, imagine the squeeze in that part of the body instead; don't skip over it.

4. Once you have worked through all the parts of the body, finish by tensing your whole body then softening into rest.

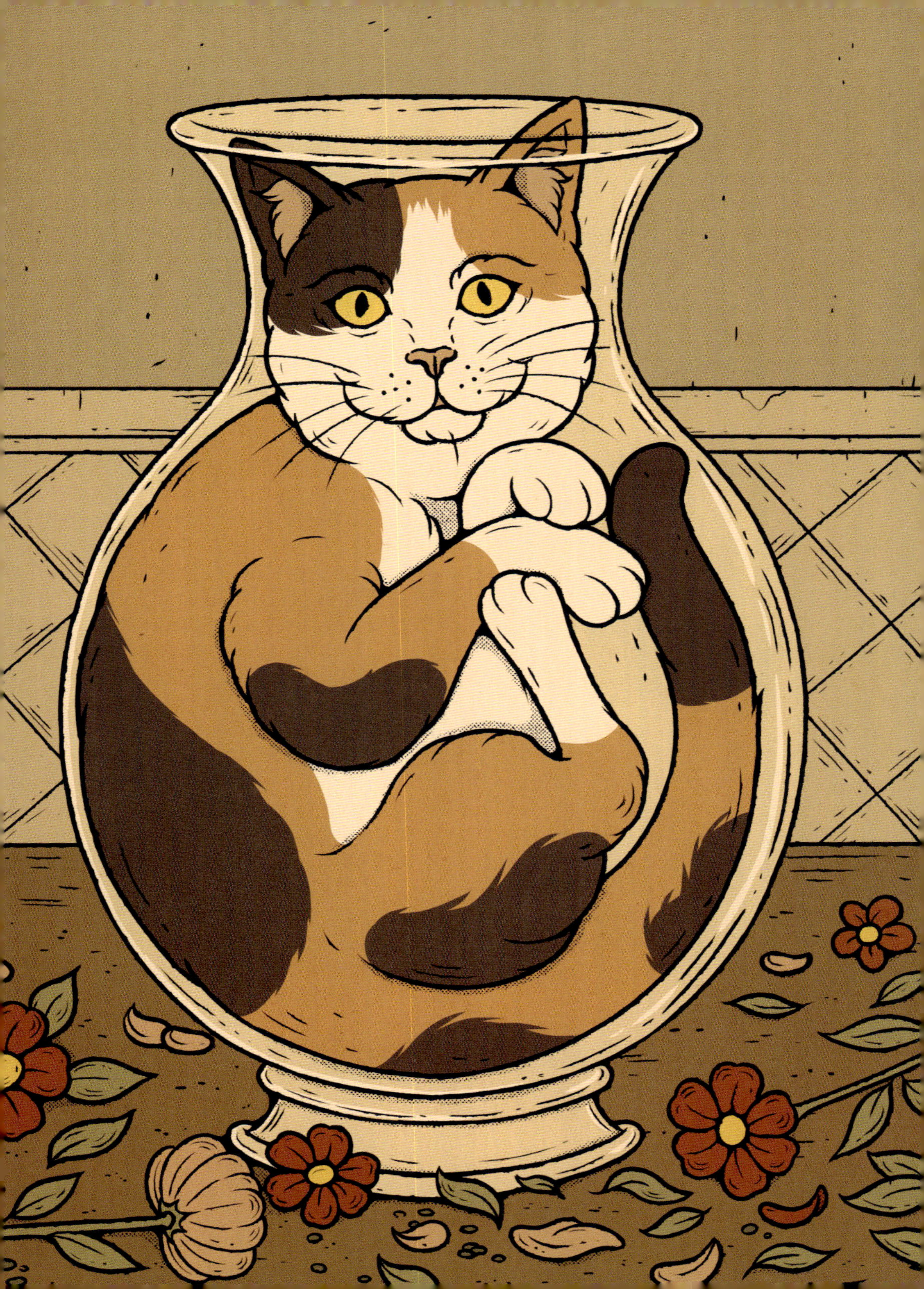

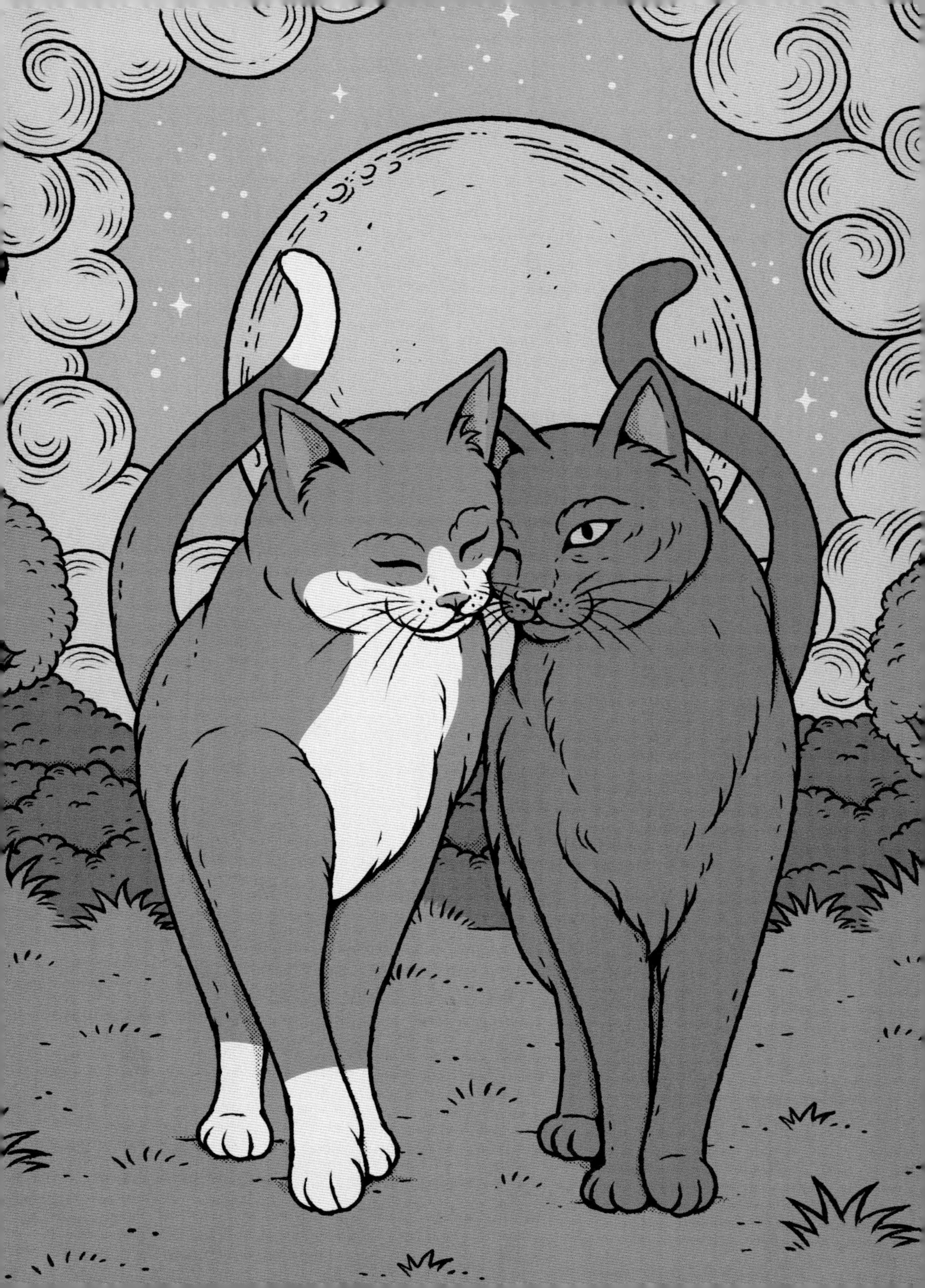

SOMATIC HUG

When the going gets tough, sometimes you just need a hug, whether from a human or a ball of fur. While some cats love being held and even hug you back, others tolerate an occasional hug, and many more outright do not enjoy a cuddle at all.

Very much like humans, cats are individuals and have their own likes and dislikes, so we don't take it personally if not all of our cats like our hugs; they simply prefer to be shown affection in a different way.

Instead we can take our cue from the independent felines and not depend on others for hugs, but learn to hug ourselves as a way of regulating our system.

This is a wonderful practice for self-soothing before bed, or whenever you need to shift anxiety.

1. Sit comfortably or lie in bed. Close your eyes or soften your gaze. Take a gentle breath in and out.

2. Cross your arms in front of your body, with your right hand resting on your left upper arm and your left hand resting on your right upper arm. Adjust as necessary to ensure this is a comfortable, relaxed hold, without any straining.

3. The hands and the arms are an energetic extension of the heart, so in this position you are wrapping yourself in the energy of the heart, in the energy of love and compassion. Hold here and give yourself a light, loving squeeze. Feel the warmth as you hold.

4. From here you can begin tapping alternate arms, for one to three minutes, so the right hand taps the left upper arm, then the left hand taps the right upper arm. Tap a slow, loose rhythm at your own pace.

5. Tuning into your breath as you continue to tap, notice if a lighter or heavier tap feels better. Keep the breath easy and natural, and imagine any tension or stress moving down and out of your body as you tap. Continue tapping until you feel a shift to having more ease in your body.

6. When you are ready to end, give yourself a soft, gentle hug. Squeeze tightly and then slow down the release from the squeeze as much as you can, allowing the brain to slowly register and record the shift in your body.

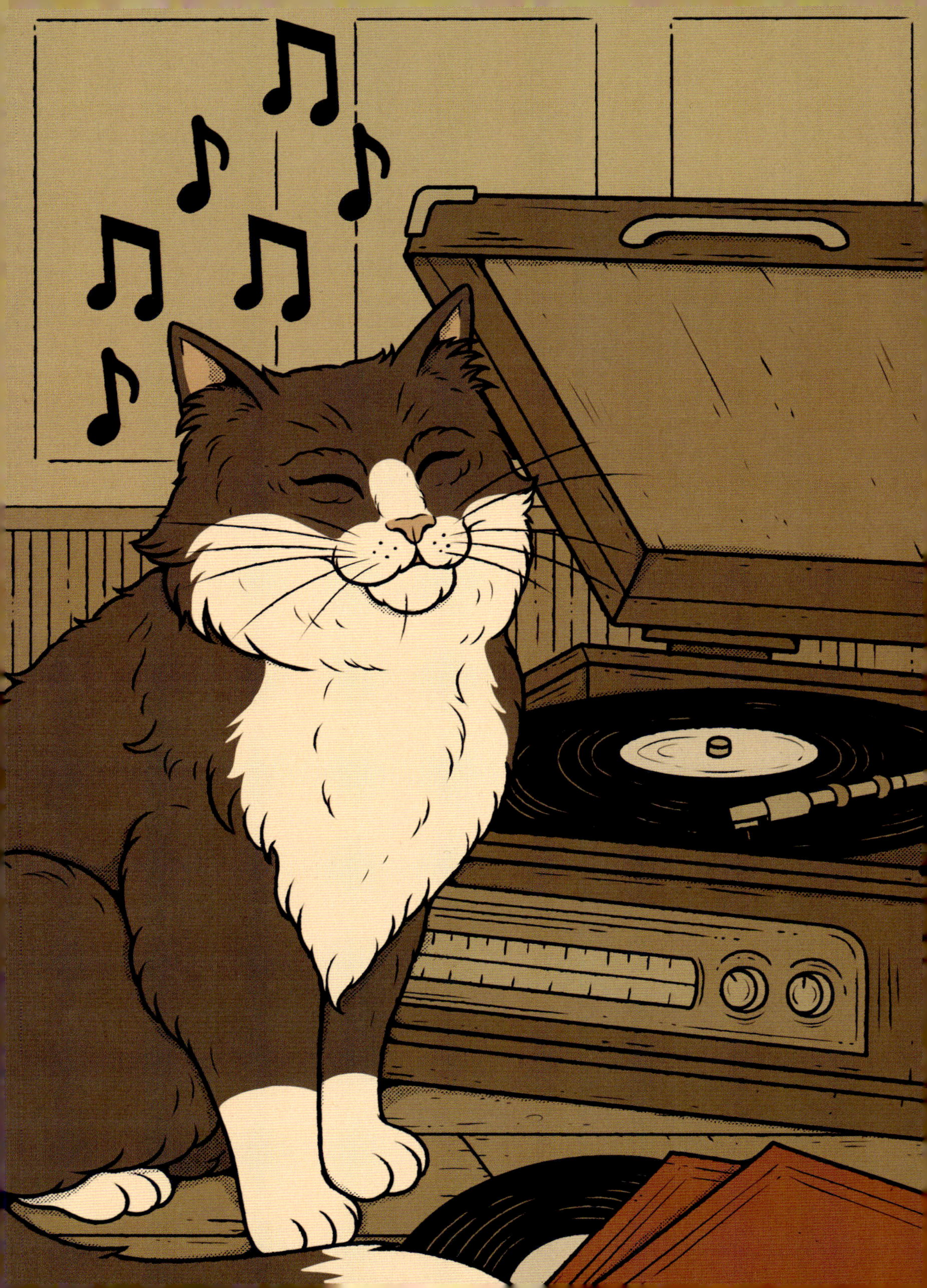

COOL CATS ABOUND

In the late 1930s and 40s, jazz musicians and club-goers were often referred to as cool cats, in reference to the self-assured, laid-back, calm nature of our feline friends. How can we be more cat and stay cool, calm, and collected in the daily chaos of life?

To approach life like a chilled-out cat, do as cats do, and sleep a lot. A good night's sleep helps us to be more resourced, regulated, and ready to meet head-on all that life brings: the good, the bad, and the in-between. When we are regulated and resourced, we approach our day unfazed by the surprises and catastrophes that come our way, and can think clearly rather than being in a constant state of reaction.

Sitali means "cooling" or "soothing" in Sanskrit, and this sitali pranayama exercise does both for the body and mind! This breath practice is especially beneficial before bedtime since it cools and grounds the body. In the same way you brush your teeth and wash your face at bedtime, you can cleanse any stress and tension from your body and your mind. You will be fresh and ready for rest on all levels!

As well as part of a good bedtime routine, this practice is a wonderful way to cool and calm heat and heated emotions in the body and system whenever you feel worked up.

1. Sit upright, comfortably, with the spine lengthened.

2. Extend your tongue out slightly past your lips while curling it up at the sides, creating a tunnel shape. If you find it difficult to curl your tongue, extend the tongue out a little past the lips with the upper lip slightly open.

3. Close your eyes or soften your gaze downward. Slowly sip the breath in through the curled tongue—or over the extended tongue—as if through a straw.

4. Now bring the tongue to press up toward the upper palate with the mouth closed and exhale through the nose.

5. Repeat Steps 3–4 for a minimum of three minutes. Feel the cooling sensation on your tongue as you sip the breath in, and know that as you tune into the coolness of the inhale you draw that coolness into your body and system, soothing any physical and emotional heat.

6. When you are ready to end, take one last cooling breath into your system, and exhale through your nose. Relax the tongue and allow the breath to be as it is. Take time to be in stillness for another minute to integrate the shifts in your system.

CAT WIGGLE

Have you ever wondered what that little butt wiggle before a cat pounces is all about? Unfortunately, not a whole lot of research has been done on this topic. However, a common theory is that cats wiggle their butts for stability and balance, a theory we can be inspired by as a way to balance and stabilize our energy.

Cats of all shapes and sizes—big ones and domesticated varieties—may also shake their butts before pouncing as a way of warming up their muscles, as well as to stretch and stabilize themselves before they push forward on the pounce. A polarity squat for a human has a similar effect, and makes a great before-bedtime practice.

This polarity squat exercise was introduced by Dr Randolph Stone, the founder of the Polarity Therapy Institute, who believed that the body, similar to the earth, has positive and negative poles and that the proper flow of energy between these poles helps us to stay healthy and balanced. Blockages and imbalance show up as issues in the physical and emotional body, and in life. A polarity squat is an excellent self-treatment posture to begin to balance energy through the body.

This posture can help to ground and stabilize your energy before bedtime for more restful sleep.

1. With feet slightly wider than hip-width apart, keep the soles fully on the ground and lower your seat down to squat in between your knees.

2. If you can do so comfortably, hold and breathe into this squat for a few minutes. If not, just shorten the time and know that the more you practice, the longer you will be able to comfortably squat.

3. If it is comfortable to do so, wrap your arms around your knees, either with the knees in the armpits as you grab onto the opposite wrist, or perhaps just holding opposite elbows.

4. From here, tuck your chin in toward your chest and gently sway back and forth for a few breaths, then sway gently from side to side for a few breaths.

5. As you continue to squat and sway, imagine that the energy through your root and your core is balancing and stabilizing. Release any imbalanced and/or stagnant energy through your legs and feet.

6. Stay in the pose for as long as it feels comfortable for you.

7. To end the pose, take a slow breath in and out and return to a standing position. Close your eyes here if it's comfortable, or soften your gaze downward, and notice the flow of energy moving through your body and your system.

ADAPTATIONS

If you need extra support, place a rolled-up towel or yoga mat under your heels.

Hold on to a chair if you need help with your balance.

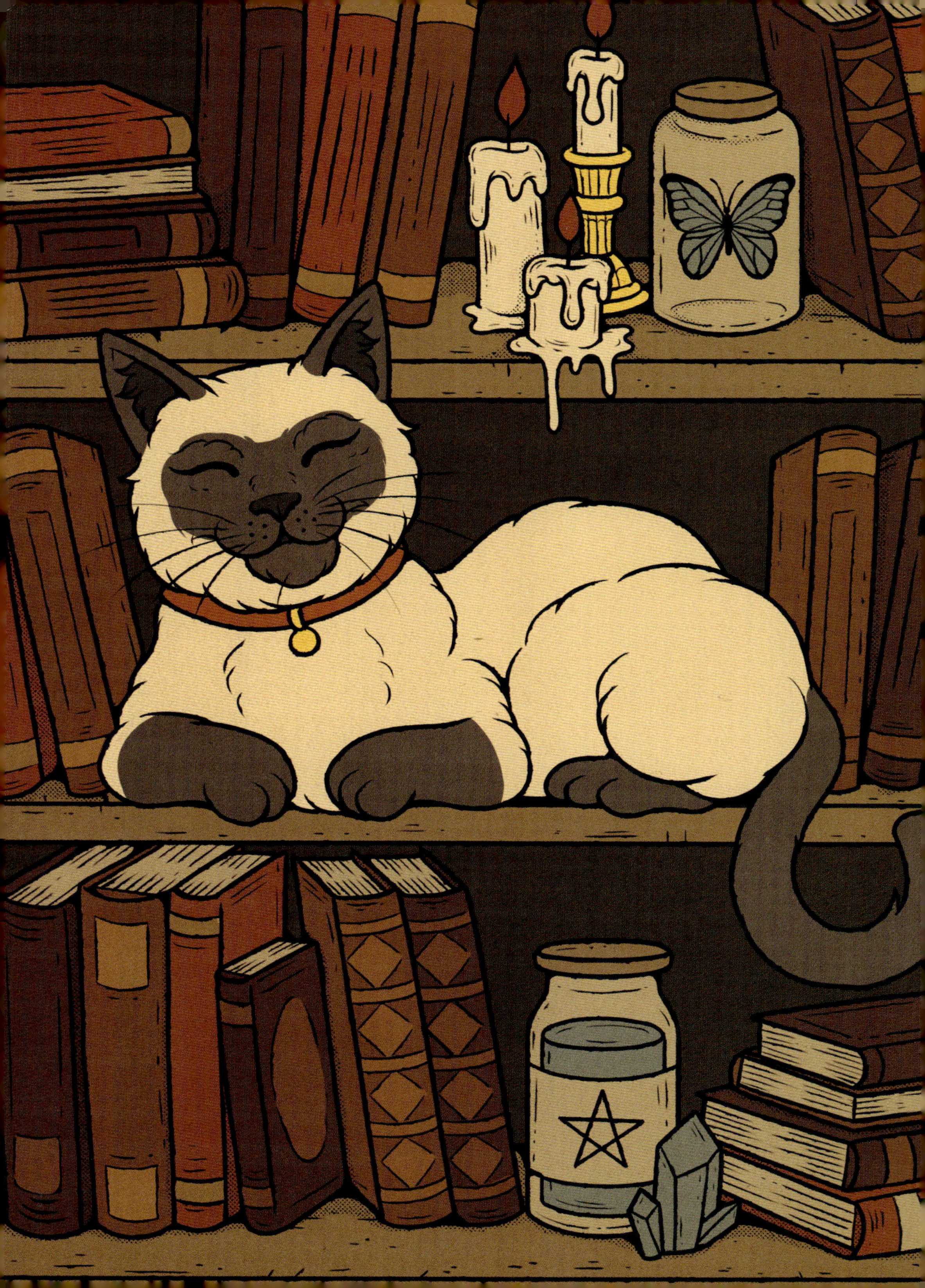

CHAPTER FIVE
JUST BE

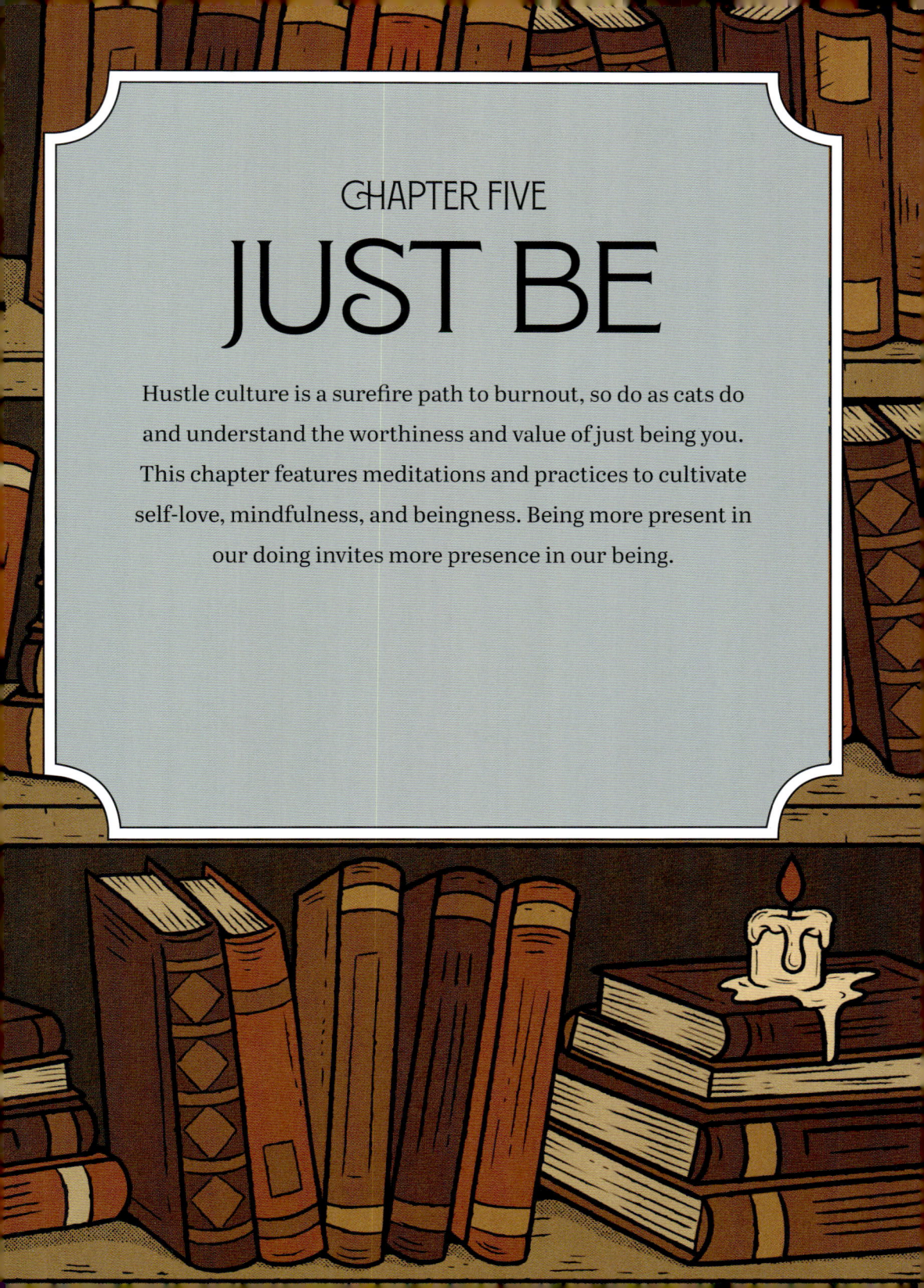

Hustle culture is a surefire path to burnout, so do as cats do and understand the worthiness and value of just being you. This chapter features meditations and practices to cultivate self-love, mindfulness, and beingness. Being more present in our doing invites more presence in our being.

> "'WHAT DAY IS IT?' ASKED POOH.
> 'IT'S TODAY,' SQUEAKED PIGLET.
> 'MY FAVORITE DAY,' SAID POOH."
>
> – A.A. MILNE

CAT TEACHINGS

COPYCAT

"What's so great about cats anyway?" a cat naysayer might ask. Well, if you don't already know, kitty certainly doesn't feel the need to persuade or sell you on how awesome they are. They know full well the power of the cat! There's no need for any convincing energy when they are simply confident in their own being.

By being copycats we too can learn from our beloved kitty companions and embrace our being. Copying is, after all, how cats learn, with kittens imitating their mothers when it comes to grooming, using the litter box, and so much more. Cats also copy humans in behavior, and mimic other kitties in postures and vocalizations to establish hierarchy and strengthen social ties. Mimicry is also a path to survival, as cats learn to take on new skills and adapt to new environments.

Since our cats are sometimes a reflection of ourselves and our own social needs, we can notice our feline companion's behavior and reflect on how that aspect might be a part of us. When we can observe and take note of kitty's internal swagger, know that we have that within ourselves as well. Simply being who we are is more than enough.

The more that you stand tall and connect to the fierce feline within, the one who knows their worth comes from just being, the more you can define success for yourself.

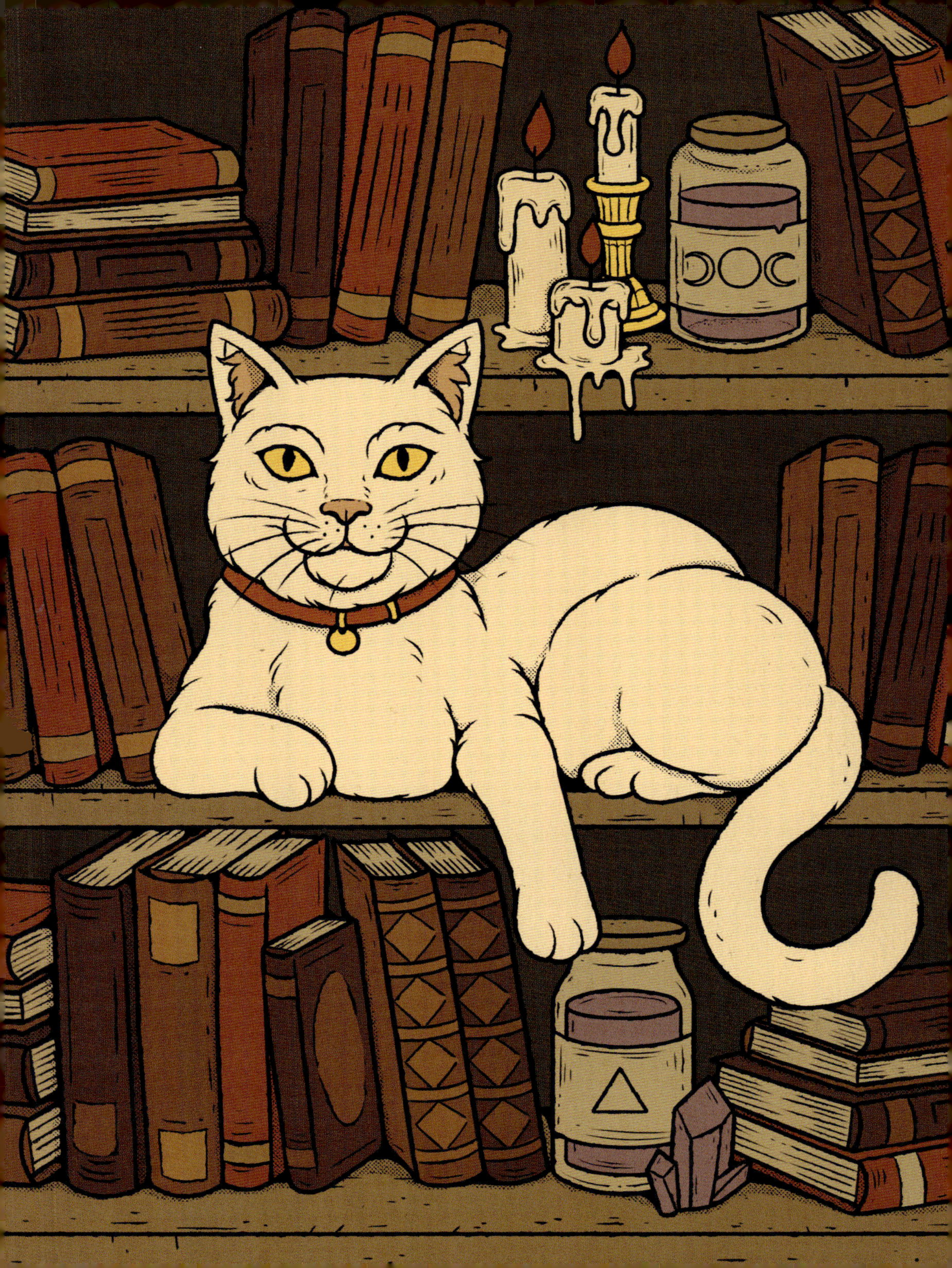

NO DOING, JUST BEING

"Goro goro" is a Japanese term that refers to the act of doing nothing, akin to simply chilling or lounging. It's appropriate as well then that "goro goro" also refers to a cat's purr!

We've established that cats are the masters of rest, but they truly have a PhD in lounging, doing nothing without shame or guilt, and simply being. Would that we were as free to relish simply lying around, but to do so represents a radical act of deconditioning since we have been taught, and have had modeled for us in the most puritanical way, that only back-breaking hard work gets results.

What if that were simply untrue? What if we chose to break from that pattern, from society's and someone else's "truth"? What if we get to redefine what success means to us and work in the unconventional way of no striving, no hustling, but rather going with the flow and simply taking action from a grounded place? If we could somehow lounge more in our internal joy, we might find success pouring in on all levels of being.

Doing nothing is a worthwhile practice to encourage you to let go of external validation and cultivate internal worth and being. In the nothingness is everything. When we operate from the stillness, we are connected to all. No resistance, no doing, just allowing, just being as you are with all that is. That is what we will begin to practice here.

Allowing yourself to be with all that is arising and nothing at all is radical practice, simply. You are opening to the flow of experience, which is simple in theory and challenging in practice. With more dedicated practice, your mind can become spacious and relaxed.

1 Sit comfortably with the back supported.

2 When sitting still, there's nothing else to do except allow whatever arises, whatever comes up. Notice if there's any kind of attachment or grasping around a thought, emotion, or sensation and simply allow it. There is no following a thought, thoughts come and go. There is nothing to do or shift or change, there is simply being with all that is.

3 Notice when your mind wants to hold onto a sensation or a thought, and in that noticing, release it, and relax into being.

4 Start with five minutes daily and build up to 11 minutes and longer. Schedule your do-nothing practice to give time in your day for your mind to be spacious.

COHERENCE BREATHING

You may have heard stories of kitties being lost on trips and traversing hundreds of miles to somehow make it back home. How is that even possible? There are animals that navigate with the magnetic field of the earth, apparently including cats!

Everything has an electromagnetic field of energy. We are all energy beings. It has been surmised that humans have vestigial traces of iron in the ethmoid bone between the eyes and nose and that we could, at some point in our evolution, tune in to the magnetic field of the earth to help guide our internal compass, just like our animal companions.

It should be no surprise then that we have electromagnetic fields around our bodies, organs, and cells. What might be surprising is that the measurable electromagnetic field of the heart is a hundred times greater than that of the brain, according to the HeartMath Institute. Yet here we are thinking that we need to figure things out by using the brain versus feeling into the heart.

This meditation, inspired by the research of the HeartMath Institute, combines visualization and breath to bring coherence through the cells of the body, since clear communication within the body makes for a healthy body and mind.

In this exercise, you will connect to your electromagnetic field and strengthen your heart space with the frequency of love, joy, and delight.

1. Sit comfortably with your eyes closed or by gazing softly downward.

2. Inhale and exhale through the nose, allowing the breath to be gentle and easy for a few rounds.

3. Now imagine receiving the in breath through your heart, then releasing the out breath through your heart. Gently and slowly imagine breathing in and out through the heart space. Slow the breath down and imagine each breath in and out strengthening the electromagnetic field of the heart.

4. Bring your mind's eye to a beloved feline companion, person, or place that brings a smile to your face when you think about them. Connect to this being or place that elicits this feeling of pure joy and delight.

5. Continue to breathe slowly in and out from your heart as you continue to connect to this sense of love and joy. Imagine each gentle inhale and exhale through the heart bringing more coherence into your body and clear communication on the deepest cellular level. The electromagnetic field of the heart can begin to align with the electromagnetic field of the brain as you continue to breathe in love and exhale even more joy into your field.

6. Remain here for three minutes to begin with, building up to 11 minutes with practice.

7. When you are ready to end, position your hands one on top of the other at the heart to seal in the joy.

ELEMENTAL BEING BREATH

In Islamic culture cats are considered ritually clean animals, and as such are allowed to roam in mosques. They are also said to possess blissful energy. Sufism is the mystical aspect of Islam, and we can draw from it a wonderful practice that reminds us of the nature around us and within us, as well as the nature that is us.

Cats were valued in the Ottoman Empire for pest control, but also due to the fact that they kept rats from destroying precious books and texts. There is a Turkish saying: "If you kill a cat, you must build a mosque." These religious and cultural beliefs have allowed for flourishing kitty populations in Turkey, and the acceptance and adoration of cats in many Islamic countries.

Hazrat Inayat Khan introduced Sufi teachings to the west in the 1900s. This simple breath with visualization practice from this mystical lineage allows you to connect to the elements of earth, water, fire, air, and ether, while at the same time connecting more deeply with your being.

This cleansing breath sequence is traditionally done daily at dawn, but you can also do it at any time in the morning to purify and clear your system in order to connect to divine wisdom and the intelligence of the universe before the start of the day. Ideally you would practice outdoors, but a good alternative is to practice while standing in front of a window.

As you focus on each element you will imagine its corresponding color and then adjust your breath accordingly:

Earth = gold
Inhale and exhale through the nose.

Water = green
Inhale through the nose and exhale through the mouth.

Fire = red
Inhale through the mouth and exhale through the nose.

Air = blue
Inhale and exhale through the mouth.

Ether = gray or transparent
Almost imperceptibly inhale and exhale through the nose.

1. Stand comfortably with a straight spine. Position your feet about hip-width apart and your arms by your sides with palms facing out. Close your eyes or soften your gaze downward.

2. Begin with the earth element. Visualize breathing the color gold in and out through the nose. As you breathe in, imagine drawing up gold-colored earth energy through your feet, through the deep rich soil of the earth, grounding, supporting, and stabilizing. As you breathe out, release the gold back down out to the earth. Complete the sequence five times in total.

3. Next is the water element. As you breathe in, slowly and gently through the nose, visualize drawing in the green water element to nourish your body and system. As you release the breath out through the mouth, imagine the green energy of water washing away anything that no longer serves you, leaving your system fresh, clean, clear, and in flow. Complete the sequence five times in total.

4. For the fire element, inhale through the mouth, visualizing red fire energy that is alchemizing and transformative in your body. As you slowly release the breath out through the nose, still visualizing that red energy, know that you are purifying and energizing your system with fire, burning through impurities. Complete the sequence five times in total.

5. As you inhale the air element through your mouth, visualize this blue energy creating expansion and expansiveness in your body and system. As you exhale through the mouth, know that in that letting go is the creation of space. Complete the sequence five times in total.

6. For the ether element, breathe in and out through the nose. Let this breath be the softest of all. Visualize a soft gray that is almost transparent and all elements mixing and meeting in the ethers, being the essence of life. Complete the sequence five times in total.

7. To end, stand in stillness and take slow, gentle breaths in and out through the nose. Bring the hands to prayer and give thanks to the elements all around us and within us.

INNER SMILE

The infamous Cheshire Cat, a character in Lewis Carroll's Alice's Adventures in Wonderland, *has a mischievous grin and the ability to disappear and reappear. He vanishes quite slowly, starting at the tip of his tail and leaving his smile on show long after the rest of him has gone.*

We can be inspired by this enigmatic feline through a Taoist meditation called inner smile. We can smile outside and inside, and let that smile linger in our bodies to reap its mental and physical benefits.

Smiling helps to release a flood of feel-good biochemicals in the body that boost the immune system, lower blood pressure, reduce pain, elevate mood, and fuel longevity. And the good news is that even if you don't feel like smiling, the physical act of smiling can still trigger that deluge of happy neurotransmitters. The Cheshire Cat was really onto something with that grin . . .

According to Traditional Chinese Medicine some organs are paired with certain emotions, which you can address with smiling:

- Liver and gallbladder for anger and resentment
- Stomach and spleen for worry and anxiety
- Kidneys and bladder for fear
- Lungs and large intestines for grief
- Heart and small intestines for lack of joy

With this practice you can share a smiling energy with your internal organs and anywhere in the body that might need it.

1. Sit in a comfortable position with chin parallel to the ground, chest open, and shoulder blades down and back. Do not hold yourself in a rigid position, but relax and build toward better posture. Close your eyes or soften your gaze downward.

2. Take a few gentle breaths in and out then, on the next inhale, let the breath fill your belly. On the exhale, squeeze the navel back toward the spine. Repeat this belly breath a few more times.

3. Softly rest the tip of the tongue on the roof of your mouth, behind your front teeth. Bring a soft, quiet smile to your lips. Continue to hold a gentle smile throughout the practice.

4 Bring a soft focus and awareness to the point between your eyebrows and imagine your smile resting there. Tune into the energy that your smile creates at the point between the brows, and feel that energy expand.

5 Use your breath to share and direct the smiling energy down into each of your organs, focusing for about one minute on each, if possible. Notice whether the organ receives the energy with resistance or ease. Remind yourself of all the benefits that come from smiling and know that these are being conferred to each organ in turn.

6 In Chinese medicine your dantian is your body's center of gravity, where it stores your qi, your life-force energy. It is located about three fingers below the navel. Just before you are ready to end, send the smiling energy to your dantian.

7 To end, release the tongue and soften your face as you release your smile. Notice your whole being uplifted on the physical, mental, and energetic levels by the energy of your smile.

MEOWFULNESS MEDITATION

How can we alleviate the mental suffering of worrying about the future or ruminating over the past? We can be present. We can be with what is in the here and now. It's the practice of mindfulness or, as it pertains to cats, "meowfulness," which teaches us to be with what is, right now in this present moment. How can we learn to be in the meow/now?

According to Buddhist tradition, we are the ones causing our own suffering. Of course, the Buddha acknowledged external pain such as illness and injustices that cause suffering. However, one of the primary causes is really our thoughts. It's quite mind-blowing when you think about it, especially if you are unfamiliar with this teaching. We suffer because of our thoughts. We have thoughts that something, someone, or some situation should be other than what it is, rather than just accepting what is. Our suffering comes from our mind.

Worrying makes us feel like we are doing something, but it just creates more anxiety and discomfort. When we bring ourselves into the present moment, we can cultivate more peace within, and more peace inside on the individual level creates more peace on the collective level. This is the practice of paying attention, noticing where your attention goes, and bringing it back time and time again to the present.

Cats are masterful when it comes to being present. We've all seen kitties lounging in their favorite, cozy spot, eyes relaxed and perfectly at peace with the world around them. This is "meowfulness." Soaking up the coziness, no intrusive thoughts, not wishing that the spot were more comfortable, just being and appreciating.

Cats are always in the now, and this exercise will help you learn how to be too.

An anchor is where your attention returns to again and again when distracted, and in this mindfulness practice we will be using breath as the anchor. You might choose other anchors, such as sounds, or sensations in the hands and feet.

1 Find a comfortable seat where you can be relaxed and alert. Close your eyes or soften your gaze downward.

2 Bring your attention to the natural movement of your breath. Consider where it might be most comfortable to rest your attention, maybe noticing the rise and fall of your chest or focusing on the sensation of air through your nostrils. Allow your attention to rest wherever it is that you notice the breath most easily, and let your breath be what it is.

3 Notice the sensation of your breath moving through that area of your body. If you find it difficult to feel the breath, place one hand in the middle of your chest and the other on your belly and physically feel the breath moving. If your attention wanders, simply come back to tracking the movement of breath in and out.

4 Start by practicing for three minutes and slowly build to 30 minutes. When you are ready to finish, take a moment to share gratitude for your awareness and know that "meowfulness" is a baseline for your day or evening.

LOVING KITTENS MEDITATION

The Buddhist loving kindness meditation, also known as metta meditation, can be practiced in a few different ways, but the core elements remain the same: wishing others and ourselves well, and by doing so cultivating more kindness and compassion for all. It's often hardest to be kind to ourselves, so in this variation on a theme, we can start with a no-brainer subject to wish well: cats!

Why is it easier to shower love on kittens than on ourselves? Why are we so hard on ourselves? Why so often do we speak unkindly to ourselves? It's most likely a survival tactic from long ago, keeping us playing small in order not to get hurt.

You and your harsh internal critic could probably use some love and compassion just about always, and this practice helps cultivate more positive feelings, starting with the ultimate feel-good cuties: kittens.

This variation on the loving kindness meditation works well with our fur babies because we love them wholeheartedly, and they us. If you don't have one in your life, imagine a trio of kittens gazing at you.

1 Sit comfortably or lie down. Close your eyes or soften your gaze.

2 Bring one hand on top of the other in the center of the chest, connecting to your heart space and the loving energy there.

3 Notice your breath and how it moves in and out. Feel the warmth of your hands on your heart space, cultivating the internal warmth of your heart.

4 Bring a kitten to your mind's eye and imagine this kitten in a way that floods your heart with love. Recite this phrase, or something similar of your own devising: *"May you be safe. May you be healthy, happy, and at ease. May you be filled with peace."*

5 Repeat three times while wrapping the kitten in this loving energy. Maintain a natural breath and notice how it feels in your body to send love, kindness, and care to this little, furry feline.

6 From here imagine yourself so that you can direct loving kindness to yourself. If you find it difficult to do this, you might imagine yourself as a small child. Better yet, imagine your child-self holding the kitten from Step 4. Again, recite this phrase or something similar: *"May you be safe. May you be healthy, happy, and at ease. May you be filled with peace."*

7 Repeat three times while wrapping your child-self and kitten in this loving energy. Notice how it feels in your body when you say these wishes out loud.

8 Repeat the process by imagining a loved one.

9 Repeat the process with a neutral acquaintance.

10 Repeat the process with someone who is challenging in your life, although only if it feels comfortable to do so. This one might be more difficult, but if you choose, perhaps imagine a child version of them that you might more easily direct loving kindness to.

11 Repeat the process with the earth.

12 When the practice and process is complete, close out by giving thanks. Notice how you feel and imagine how spacious and light-filled your heart space now is.

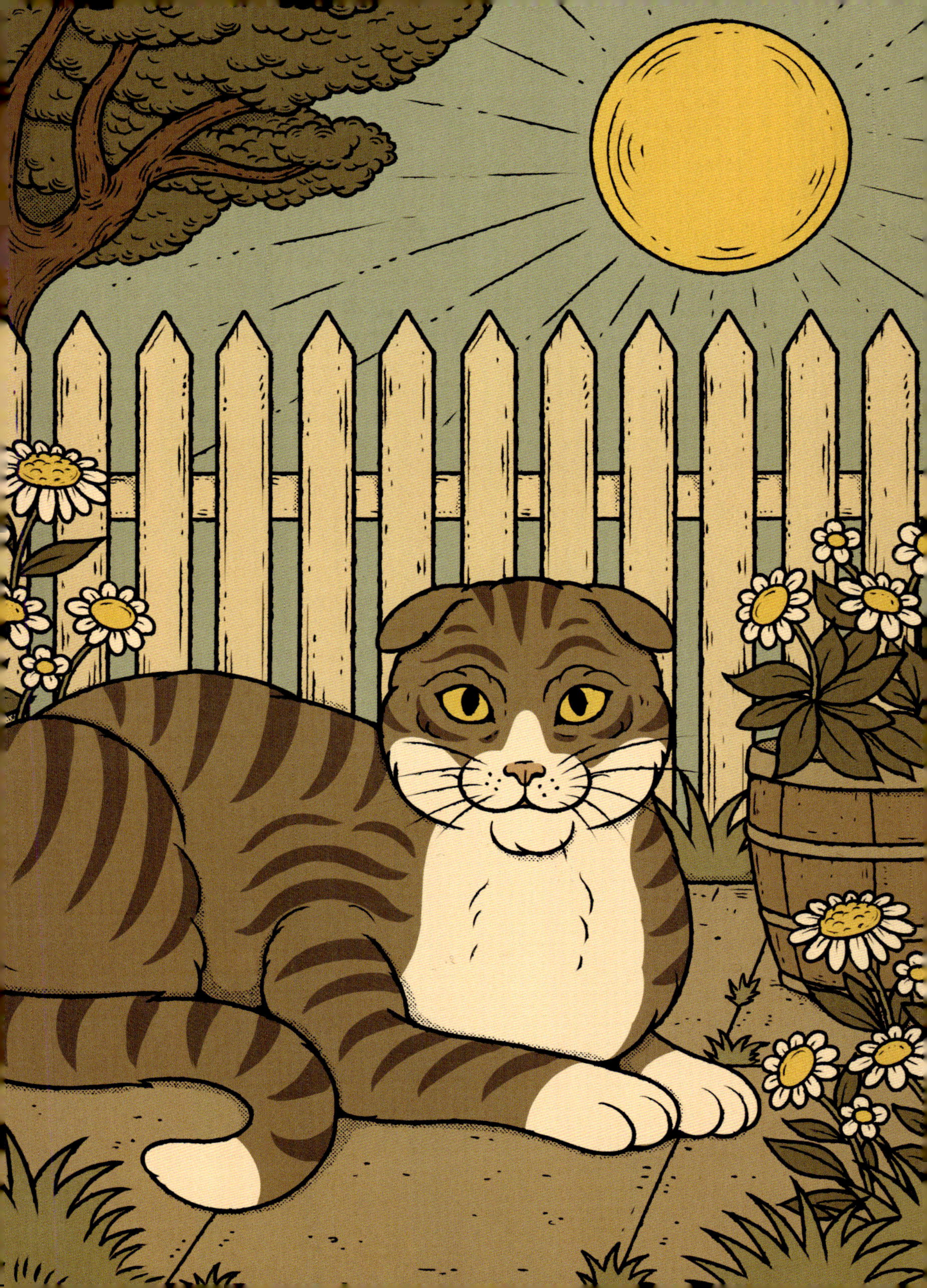

BASK IN LOVE

Kitties great and small love to bask in the sunshine, because cats love the warmth. Sitting in a sunny spot means they don't have to generate any of their own energy to stay warm, instead they conserve energy by utilizing other heat sources. Such clever kitties!

Sunlight exposure produces serotonin in both animals and humans, which regulates mood and helps everyone feel good. In the same way kitties bask in the sunshine to gain warmth and all the feel-good vibes, we can activate our own internal joy generator. This somatic healing meditation is inspired by the work of Donna Eden and her radiant circuit practices which are based on Traditional Chinese Medicine's extraordinary vessels, reservoirs of subtle energy.

You can start and end each day with this exercise, and the more you practice the more joy you'll rediscover within and around you.

1. Sit comfortably, upright yet relaxed.

2. Tuck your hands into the opposite armpits with the thumbs sticking out, so the arms crisscross across the chest. Relax in this position; there should be no tensing or straining.

3. Inhale for a slow count of five through the nose, and exhale for a slow count of five through the nose. You will continue for three minutes minimum, and build to as long as you like. Feel the softening of any tension or stress in the body as you rest your system.

4. With the hands tucked in, imagine that you are plugging yourself back into yourself, calm and resourced. Plugging your energy system back in to be charged, plugging back into love and joy and feeling resourced with energy and radiance.

5. When you are ready to close, slowly release the hands down to rest. Sit quietly and notice how and what you are feeling.

SOOTHING ENERGY HEAD HOLD

In Beatrix Potter's The Tale of Samuel Whiskers or The Roly Poly Pudding, *Tom Kitten disobeys his mother and ends up being caught and prepared as a meal by a rat couple, who smear him with butter and wrap him up tightly in dough.*

Being prepared as a meal doesn't sound much fun, but being held or rolled up like a burrito is calming for the nervous system—similar to the effect of an anxiety-reducing dog shirt or the comfort of a weighted blanket. This easy practice is adapted from an energy kinesiology therapy called Touch for Health, and might be the human version of a calming "purrito," when kitties need to be bundled up to receive medicine or get their nails trimmed. Anytime you are anxious or upset, use this hold for a few minutes to regulate your system by processing and defusing distress.

Use this practice anytime you wish to reset and restore your system from upset and stress.

1. Sit comfortably. Consider an issue, memory, sensation, or emotional upset. On a scale of one to ten, one being the least charged and ten being the most charged, rate the issue or memory.

2. Place one hand lightly on your forehead with the pinky finger across the eyebrows and thumb by the hairline. Hold the back of your head with the other hand, by the base of the skull.

3. Gently focus on the distress or issue as you breathe long and slow. Feel the warmth of your hands bringing coherence, balance, and calm to your brain.

4. Remain in this position for around two to five minutes, until you experience a calmness within. You may notice a light pulsation in both hands, or perhaps just the warmth as the energy around the issue shifts and releases.

5. When you are ready to come out, slowly release the hands down to rest. Check back in on the issue and the number you are experiencing it at now. Notice how the number has shifted.

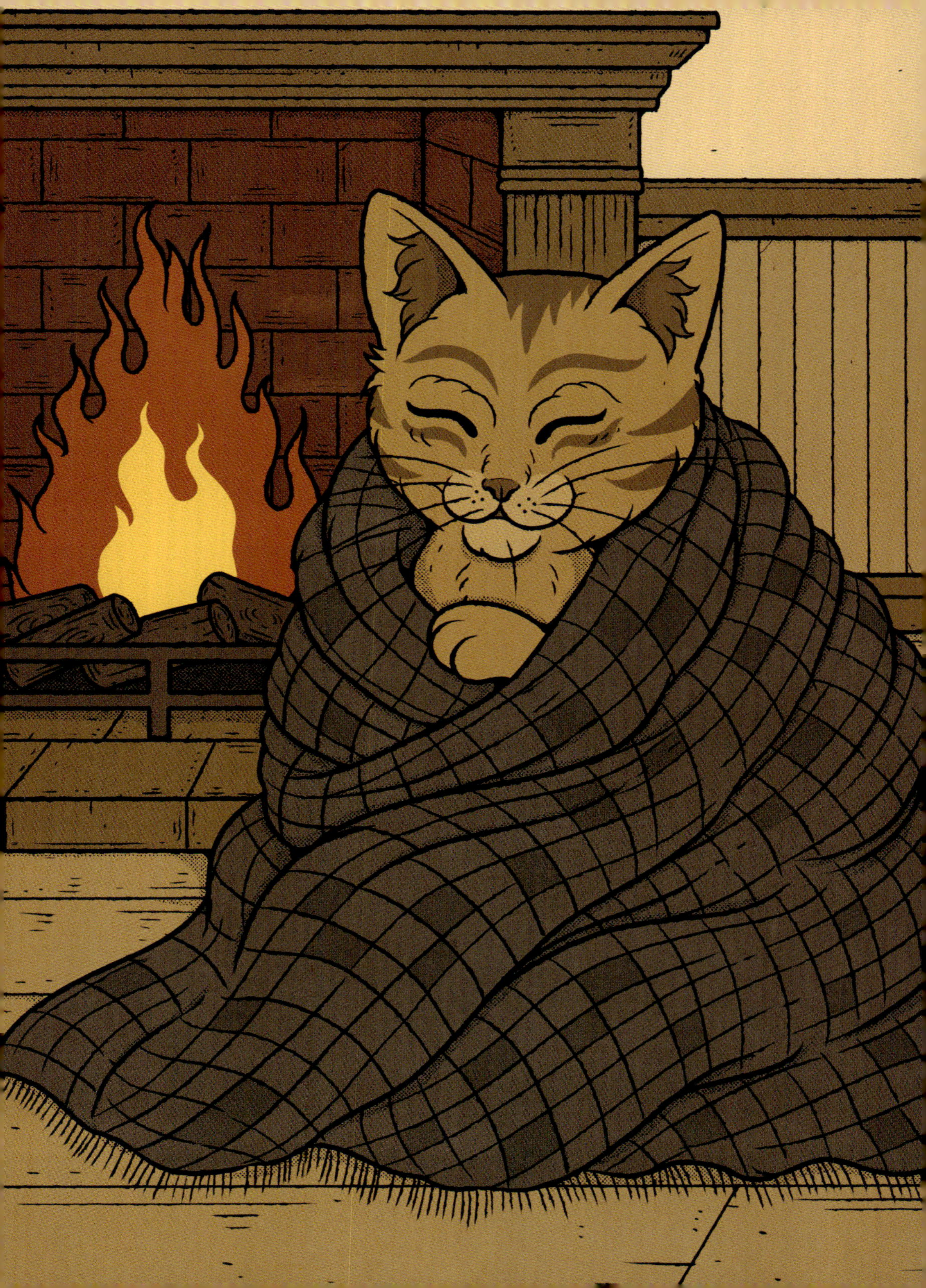

MUDRA TO ACTIVATE FELINE WISDOM

The wisdom of cats lies in their presence and their ability to be present. There is no anxiety or worry, they are resting when they rest and spontaneous in their play. Throughout this book we learn from the behaviors of cats, and in this sense they are our kitty sages.

In statues and paintings we often see the bodhisattvas (an individual who is on the path toward becoming a buddha) and Eastern sages holding the gyan mudra, which translates from the Sanskrit into "wisdom seal." It comes from a long lineage of spiritual knowledge, so you might say that holding the gyan mudra is a way of receiving the wisdom of the ages, and of the kitty sages.

The more we relax, the more we can receive, and for this posture the palms face up in order to receive.

1. Sitting quietly and comfortably, close your eyes or soften your gaze downward.

2. Bring the tip of the thumb to touch the tip of the index finger, forming a circular shape, with the remaining fingers extending out together and the palm facing up. The hold should be firm but not distracting,

3. Do this with both hands, palms up, resting on your thighs.

4. Breathing gently and with ease, invite your body to relax with each inhale and exhale. Start with five to ten rounds of gentle breathing. Release and relax with your breath as you hold this seal, and feel the sensations in your body. Imagine that your system is infused with wisdom, and trust that through intentionally taking the time to sit quietly, knowledge gets to be processed through the body. Let wisdom be the felt sense in your body.

5. To end, simply release the hands and close in gratitude for the lineage of spiritual wisdom.

KITTY MUDRA

There is a mudra called citta *which refers to the mind in Sanskrit, and this mudra helps us to awaken our consciousness. Hence, we can rename it "Kitty Mudra," because kitties are an excellent reminder of what it's like to be present, mindful, and aware.*

Activating the present that is your presence is the key to emulating kitty consciousness, and this practice is an easy way to boost mindfulness and tune into being.

The more you practice this mudra, the more it works for you, and the state becomes anchored into your system through regular use.

With practice, you learn to hold this mudra for just one breath to instantly shift your state from overwhelm and anxiety to being more present.

1. Sit upright in a position that is comfortable.

2. Bring the hands to prayer at the center of the chest. Press the index finger pads together as you bend and bring them toward the thumbs so they also touch the pads of index fingers. Keep the remaining fingers extended and touching.

3. With this mudra held at the heart, you are breathing more consciousness and awareness into the heart space. Since this is a mudra for the mind, being held at the heart, we have heart and brain connection, and when we breathe slowly with intention while activating the energy of this mudra, we have clear and present communication between heart and mind.

4. Relax into this mudra as you breathe long and deep for three minutes or longer, each breath in and out creating more awareness and presence. When you are ready to finish, release the mudra and take a moment to notice how and what you are feeling now.

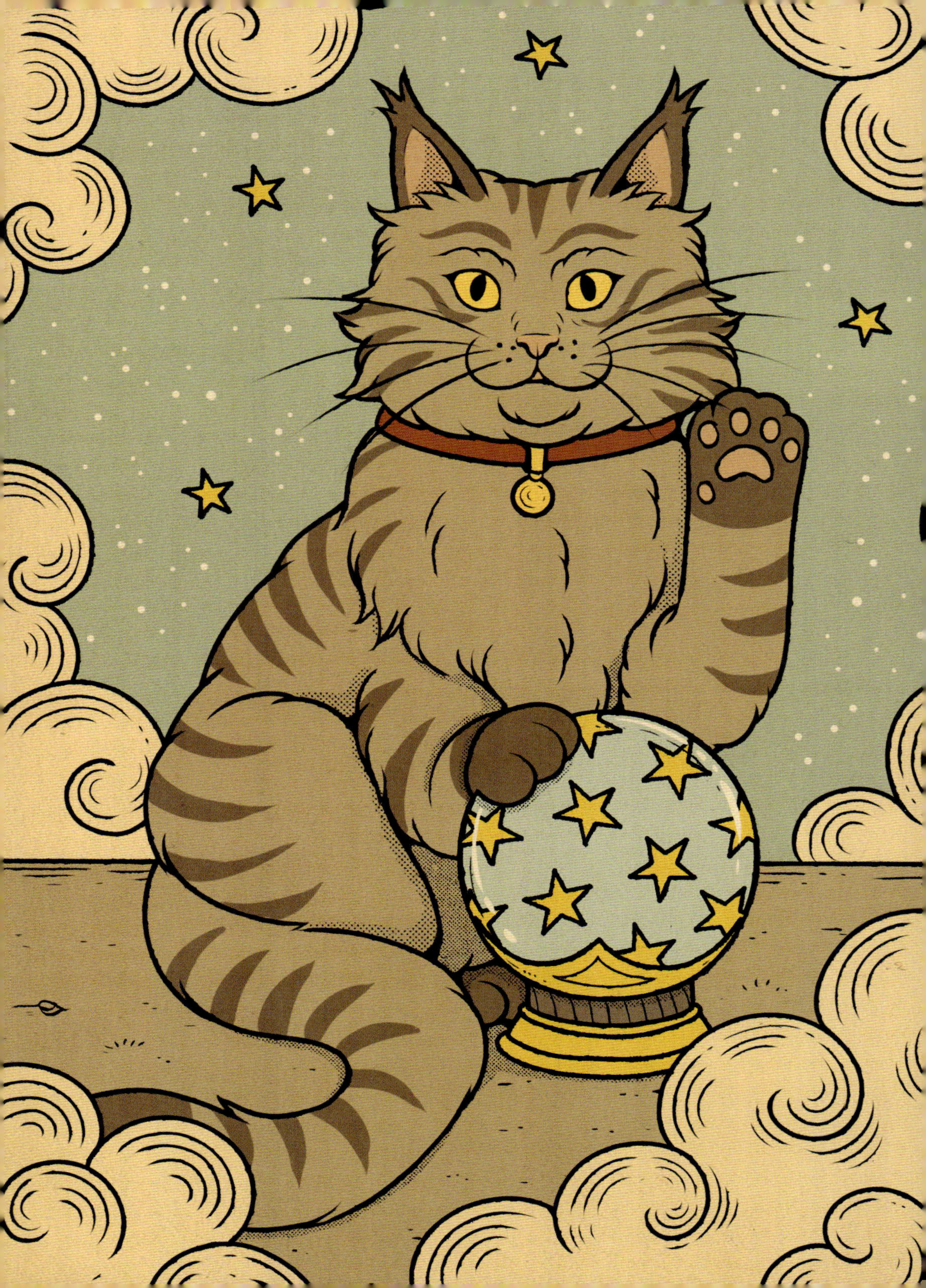

OUTRO

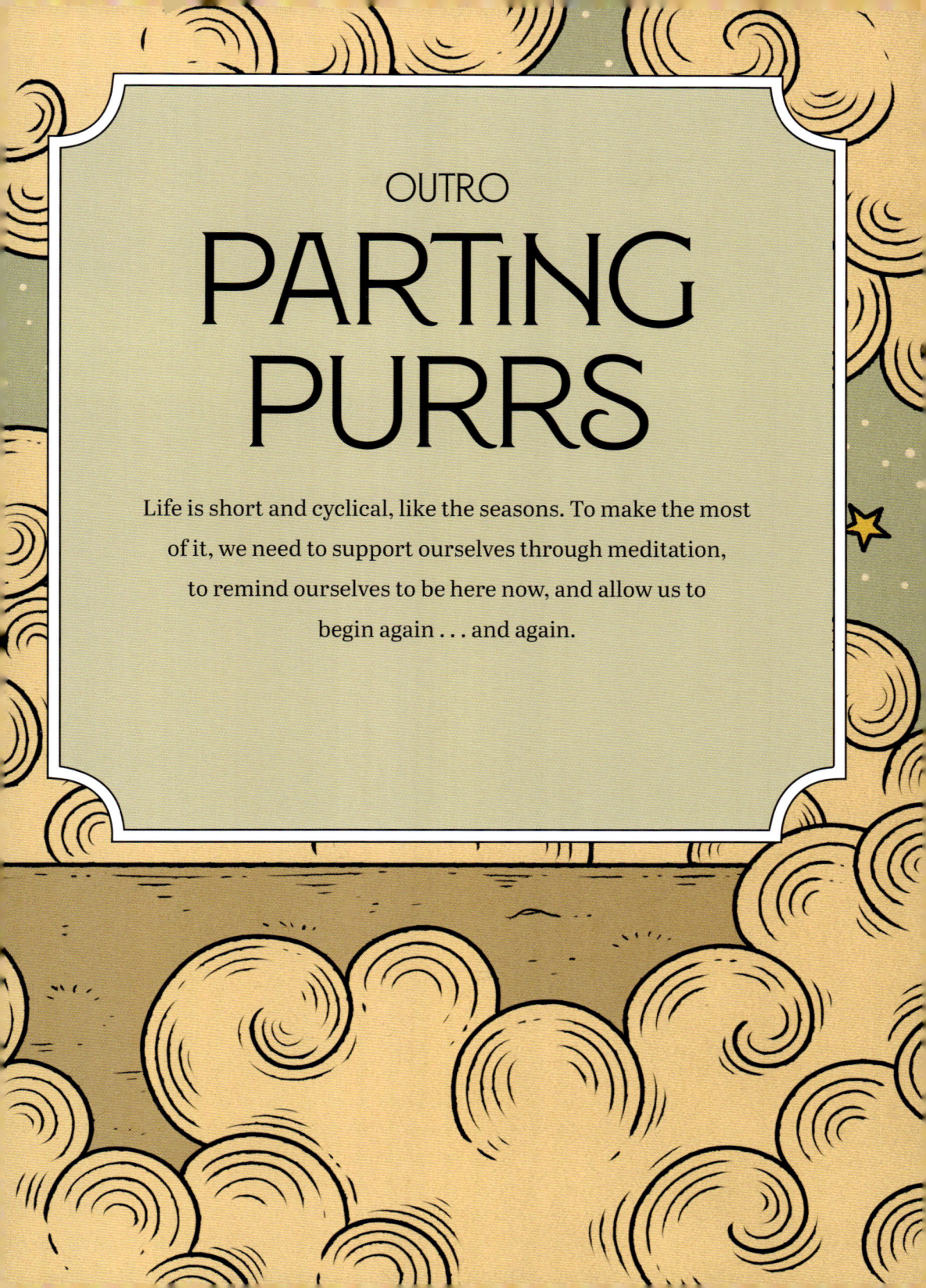

PARTING PURRS

Life is short and cyclical, like the seasons. To make the most of it, we need to support ourselves through meditation, to remind ourselves to be here now, and allow us to begin again . . . and again.

"**MEDITATION MEANS TO LOOK DEEPLY, TO TOUCH DEEPLY, SO WE CAN REALIZE WE ARE ALREADY HOME.**"

– THÍCH NHẤT HẠNH

CAT TEACHINGS

PAWS & PAUSE

As much as we wish that our cats truly had nine lives, it's sadly just the one, and the hurt and grief when you lose a feline companion is great. It is simply the price we pay for having loved and been loved.

What a gift to have known and loved a cat. To have had the experience of unconditional love from the sweetest, furry being. A gift to have held them in your arms. To nuzzle into their warm, soft, fluffy body. To love so very deeply means that the hurt of loss will be great. It's simply the price we pay for extraordinary, unconditional love. Loss is exquisitely painful, but the love you share never dies. If grief has made itself known, old or new, welcome it. Allow it space to be. Let it arise from the depths of your being where it may have been pushed down or hidden away.

When some time has passed, when the edge has softened on the intensity of loss, you might begin to mine the depths of this extraordinary thing called grief. Because when you can delve into the deepest, darkest corners of your grief, you will come away with buried treasure. This treasure that has always been there. Invaluable treasure that can never be lost, because once you have experienced love in its many forms, it remains with you and is forever a part of the fabric of your being.

Spiritual teacher Ram Dass said that we are all walking each other home. To come home one day with furry beloveds no longer around to greet you is painful, but your beloved feline has created a forever home in your heart, where they live out the rest of their nine lives in your memories as we live out ours.

Love and grief go hand in paw. There's no way around it. If you haven't met it yet, you will. Even more reason to savor this time together.

HO'OPONOPONO FOR FORGIVENESS

Cats don't hold grudges. We shouldn't either. At the end of our time together, however long or short, forgiveness is how we make space for more love and continued joy.

This mantra from Hawaiian shamanic wisdom centers on a reconciliation practice. The idea is that we get to take responsibility for what comes into our consciousness, and by repeating these phrases we help to clear, balance, and harmonize energy.

Repeat this mantra to yourself at any time, and anywhere.

1. Bring to mind a situation or an issue that makes you feel hopeless, powerless, guilty, or that feels painful.

2. Repeat silently to yourself, over and over:

   I'm sorry.
   Please forgive me.
   I love you.
   Thank you.

3. You don't have to believe these words for them to have a cleansing effect, but it does work better if you can find some small part that is true for you.

LUCKY CAT MEWDRA

In the end lies the beginning. At the beginning of this book we heard the story of the lucky cat maneki-neko, *and we wrap up our time together with the practice of the lucky cat.*

In the Japanese origin story, the *maneki-neko* beckoned the nobleman to the safety of the temple, where he was protected from a violent storm outside.

The figurine itself, with its upraised paw, is not dissimilar to representations of Hindu deities, the Buddha, and bodhisattvas holding the abhaya mudra to instill fearlessness and resilience.

The fear of loss and grief might prevent us from wanting to love or care for a companion kitty or anyone else ever again. This mudra reassures and provides a sense of safety to open your heart and take courage to do the things that you've been putting off because of fear. This cat mudra also reminds us all to follow our hearts, have faith, and to rest easy, knowing that we are divinely guided.

In this practice, we use the abhaya mudra hold as an energetic activation of security, courage, and luck.

1. Sit comfortably and take a gentle breath in and out.

2. Raise your right hand to chest height with the palm facing out, fingers together and pointing straight up. The hand should be relaxed and firm but not rigid. Rest the left hand in your lap.

3. Breathe long, slow, and deep, and hold this mudra for three to 11 minutes as you shift anxiety and fear. Think of the lucky cat projecting a shield of energy—for safety, courage, and abundance—from your right palm and circling your whole body and being.

4. When you are ready to come out, release the hands to rest, and give thanks to the power and prosperity of the *maneki-neko* activated within you!

INDEX

A
"ack ack ack ack" sound 50–1
adaptations 56, 60, 63, 73, 87, 97
anchors 110
appreciation 28–9
asanas 60–3
awareness, breath 12–13

B
bedtime routine 90, 95, 97
bee breath 34–5
being, just 102–3
Bhramari pranayama 34–5
bija mantras 38, 48
blinks, slow 88–9
blue light/energy 39
box breathing 80–1
Buddhism 15, 20, 43-4, 110, 112–13, 118, 125

C
candle gazing 18–19
cat gazing 26–7
cat king mudra 48–9
cat-cow asana 60–1
catnaps 78–9
catwalk 58–9
chakras 38–9, 48, 60
chandra nadi pranayama 84
chanting 38, 42–3, 50
citta mudra 119
cleansing breath sequence 107
coherence breathing 104–5
"cooling" 94–5
copycat 100–1

cosmic cats 20
cymatics 40

D
dance & shake 66–7
Dass, Ram 123

E
elemental being breath 106–7
expanded awareness 16–17
eye gazing 22–3
eye press 82–3

F
flower gazing 24–5
4/8/8 breathing exercise 13
frequencies, feline 32–3
fun, feline 54–5

G
gazing deeply 22–3
gemstones 38
gratitude 28–9
grief, love and 123–5
gyan mudra 15, 118

H
Hakalau practice 16
happy kitten 62–3
head hold, soothing energy 116–17
healing, sound 40–1
heart chakra 48
Hinduism 15, 43–4, 125
hissing 36–7, 70–1
Ho'oponopono mantra 124

hug, somatic 92–3
humming 34, 38, 46–7
hunters, kitty 50–1

I
Inayat Khan, Hazrat 106
inner smile 108–9
inspiration, feline 7
internal organs 108

J
jumping jacks 56–7
Jainism 43

K
kapota mudra 50
kindness meditation 112–13
kinesiology, applied 75
kitty asana 63
kitty curl and arch 64–5
kitty gazing 26–7
kitty mudra 119

L
laughter 90
lion's breath 68–9
love and grief 123–5
lucky cat 6, 125
lunar breath 84–5

M
magnetic field 104–5
maneki-neko 6, 125
mantras 44–5, 50, 124
meditative walking 58
meowfulness meditation 110–11

metta meditation 112–13
mindfulness 110
mudras 15, 42, 48–9, 118–19

N
negative thoughts 44
nervous system 83
nostril breathing, alternate 14–15
nothing, doing 102–3

O
observations, feline 11
"om shanti om" mantra 50

P
parasympathetic nervous system 16, 34, 42, 75, 86
paschimottanasan 86
paws, extended 86–7
Peripheral Vision Technique 16–17
play, feline 54–5
polarity squat 96–7
positive thoughts 44
pranayama practices 12, 14, 34–5, 80–1, 84
progressive relaxation 90–1
pspspsps sound 33
purr vibrations 46–7
purring 34, 103

R
relaxation, progressive 90–1
retention, breath 14

S
seated forward bend pose 86
seed mantras 38, 48
shake, dance & 66–7
shamanism 124
"shhhhhh" sound 70
sky gazing 20–1
slow blinks 88–9
smile, inner 108–9
solar plexus chakra 60
somatic eye press 82–3
somatic healing meditation 115
somatic hug 92–3
"soothing" 94–5
soothing energy head hold 116–17
sound healing 40–1
square breathing 80–1
Sufism 106
sunlight exposure 114–15
suspension, breath 14

T
Tai Chi 72
Taoism 24
tapping 74
throat chakra 38–9
tiger pose 72–3
Traditional Chinese Medicine (TCM) 70, 74, 108, 115
trataka meditation 18–19
2/4/4 breathing exercise 13

V
vagus nerve 75
venom breath, blowing out the 70–1
vibrations, purr 46–7

W
wiggle, cat 96–7
wisdom, feline 118

Y
yawn, full-body 64
yogic traditions 18, 42, 60–1, 68, 84

ACKNOWLEDGMENTS

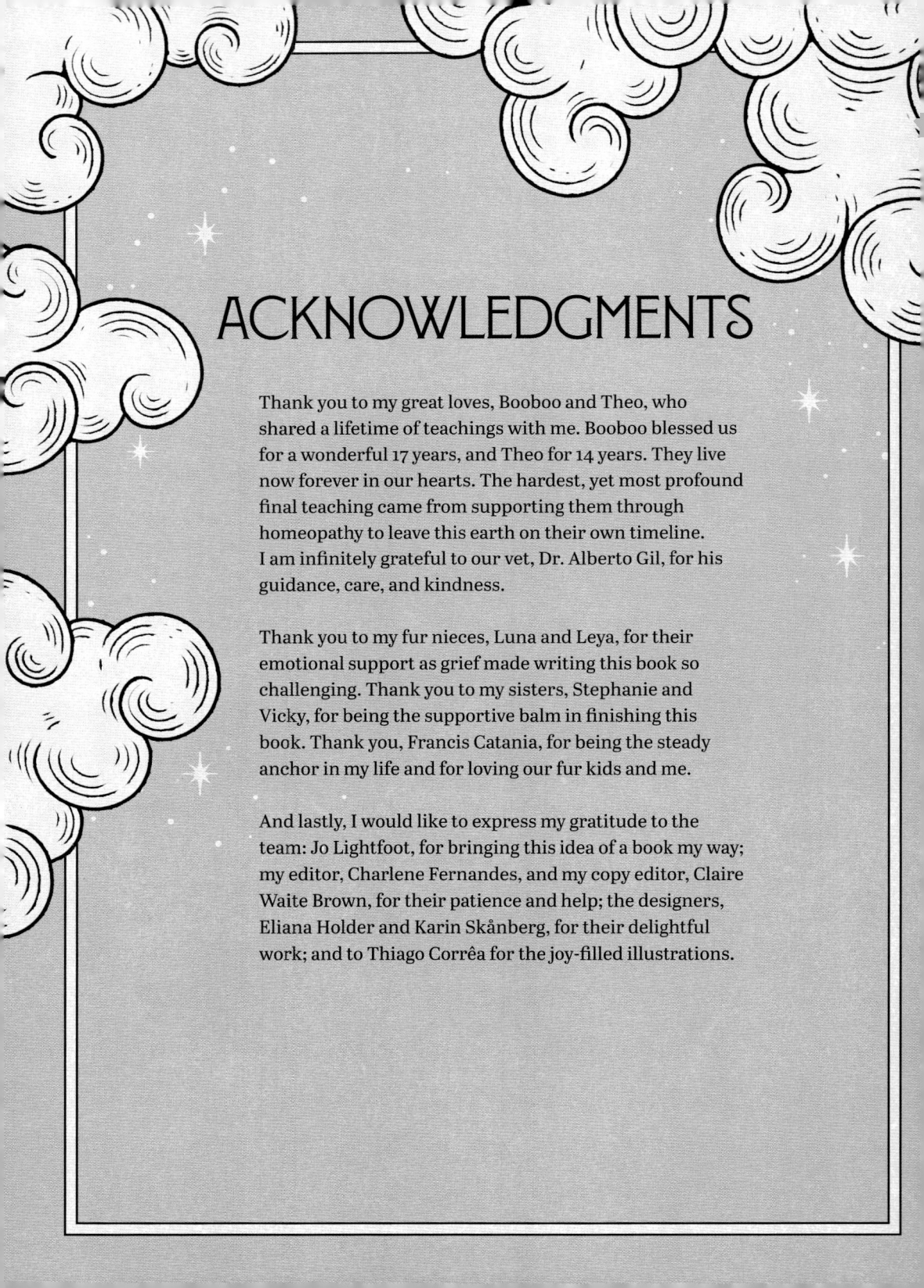

Thank you to my great loves, Booboo and Theo, who shared a lifetime of teachings with me. Booboo blessed us for a wonderful 17 years, and Theo for 14 years. They live now forever in our hearts. The hardest, yet most profound final teaching came from supporting them through homeopathy to leave this earth on their own timeline. I am infinitely grateful to our vet, Dr. Alberto Gil, for his guidance, care, and kindness.

Thank you to my fur nieces, Luna and Leya, for their emotional support as grief made writing this book so challenging. Thank you to my sisters, Stephanie and Vicky, for being the supportive balm in finishing this book. Thank you, Francis Catania, for being the steady anchor in my life and for loving our fur kids and me.

And lastly, I would like to express my gratitude to the team: Jo Lightfoot, for bringing this idea of a book my way; my editor, Charlene Fernandes, and my copy editor, Claire Waite Brown, for their patience and help; the designers, Eliana Holder and Karin Skånberg, for their delightful work; and to Thiago Corrêa for the joy-filled illustrations.